BEAUTIFUL BARGELLO

BEAUTIFUL BARGELLO

26 CHARTED BARGELLO AND NEEDLEPOINT DESIGNS

Joyce Petschek

Trafalgar Square Publishing

DEDICATION

This book is dedicated with love and extraordinary appreciation to Carla Petschek
for her unquestioning helpfulness, her superb stitching and her remarkable knowledge
about tapestries and textiles.

First published in the United States of America in 1997
by Trafalgar Square Publishing,
North Pomfret, Vermont 05053

First published in Great Britain in 1997
by Collins & Brown Limited

Printed and bound in the United States

1 3 5 7 9 8 6 4 2

ISBN: 1-57076-093-4

Library of Congress Catalog Card Number: 97-60006

Editor: Gillian Haslam
Designer: Janet James
Photography: Heini Schneebeli

Reproduction by Centre Media

PREVIOUS PAGE: *As in traditional designs, here a vertical background bargello pattern is
combined with the flexibility of long and short stitches whose curves define the abstract yellow flower.
Its complementary colors of yellow and purple with magenta create an intense and dramatic
effect as the yellow comes forward and purple with magenta recedes.*

Contents

THE LEGENDS AND HISTORY OF BARGELLO

*D*URING THE FOURTEENTH CENTURY a particular needlework style emerged whose origin seems as complicated as the extensive patterns available within it. Its precise lineage is veiled in nostalgic legends and confusion abounds from the use of the three names to describe it – Bargello, Florentine embroidery and Hungarian Point embroidery.

According to documents dating from the late fourteenth century, Princess Jadwiga of Hungary married the Polish King, Vladislav V of the Jagiello family, also spelled Jagello. Accomplished in Hungarian Point embroidery, Jadwiga stitched works for the church and the crown, leading some to believe that the technique was known by her husband's name, Jagiello, later Bargello as it is known today.

A second reference concerns a Hungarian princess who married into the Italian Medici family. As needlework accompanied such noblewomen wherever they resided and, as her trousseau was extensively embroidered, it has been assumed that she taught the ladies of the Florentine court the art of *punto ungero*, or Hungarian Point.

A third legend speaks of Elizabeth of Hungary who, during times when wool was short, supposedly taught this economical use of stitches to those in need. Later, in the eighteenth century, this stitch became a favorite of Queen Maria Teresa whose work is preserved in the Hungarian National Museum.

LEFT: *Harmony and complementary effects can be created when juxtaposing diverse patterns with similar color schemes. The art of bargello encourages imaginative play with patterns, placing unlikely designs next to one another, so that when similar colors join together, they create effects that are both exciting and compatible.*

Through coincidence, further confusion concerns the Florentine thirteenth-century Bargello Palace, built by the noble Podesta family. In the sixteenth century it became the residence of the chief of police, as well as being a political prison for men condemned to die. After extensive renovation in 1865, as the Bargello Museum it listed amongst its furniture inventory four seventeenth-century armchairs with this type of stitching. In 1886 another seven chairs from the same period whose backs and seats were covered in

punto ungero were purchased, these chairs perhaps being its association with bargello needlework.

From this interwoven history it is not surprising that over the centuries the terms bargello, Florentine embroidery and Hungarian Point have been interchanged to describe similar types of needlework. However, while Florentine embroidery and Hungarian Point both refer to specific stitchwork, the term bargello seems to indicate the patterns created from this stitchery, an accepted name for generations covering the many variations of its fascinating designs.

Particularly since the late sixteenth century, this exquisite canvaswork was used to create beautiful and practical textiles, for bed and wall hangings where rooms were draughty, for upholstered furniture, chairs, fender stools and footstools. The canvas pieces from the late sixteenth and seventeenth centuries were often large with decorative table coverings measuring over 5 m (18 feet) in length and up to 1.8 m (6 feet) in width, while small items included shoes, knife sheaths, pin cushions, purses and boxes for toiletries.

Floral motifs were frequently interlaced with these geometric patterns, combining silk threads and wool on fine gauze-like canvas. From the late seventeenth century until the mid-eighteenth century, bargello panels were wall mounted as an alternative to silk wall coverings and were often stretched on free-standing screens, firescreens and handscreens.

The technique waned in the nineteenth century, later to be revived in the United States during the 1960s and 1970s when it was enhanced by a diversity of colors and further definition of design.

In essence, bargello is a beautiful needlework technique whose structured pattern is formal, elegant and graceful. Consisting of straight stepped stitches, one established pattern is repeated in different color sequences throughout the canvaswork. Rather than pictorial designs, bargello motifs are geometric in design, classic patterns of visual balance and order. While the pattern itself is linear, its fluidity is achieved through color. Selected color shadings and variations so alter the design that harmonious or dramatic effects result from color combinations as much as from the upright stitch itself.

During its fluid history bargello has assimilated stitches and incorporated designs from many countries. Yet its many combinations of stitch lengths with infinitesimal possibilities for patterns weighs equally with its potential enrichment from using intense color tonalities and the extraordinary varieties of threads available for the creative imagination. An exceedingly personal form of needlework, in bargello the stitcher chooses color tones which inspire the imagination much as the painter works with his palette. This unique relationship between color and texture also reflects its emotional content, enhancing the meaningfulness of each bargello project stitched.

NEUTRALS

$\mathcal{T}$HE NEUTRAL COLORS of brown and grey, rather then being symbolic in themselves, serve as background tones, creating harmony or acting as contrast for other colors. Browns, known for rustic simplicity, are familiar in oak beams, scrubbed pines and mahogany panelled walls. Brownies were guardian spirits protecting brown woods, known in folk tales as the 'little people'. In legend, grey was the color between the worlds, denoting lost love. Its color of ashes meant the fire of love had been extinguished, so the maiden remained in the grey mist until her desire for life returned.

NEUTRALS

*"While painting it I said to myself: I must not
go away before there is something of an autumn evening air
about it, something mysterious, something serious."*

VINCENT VAN GOGH, LETTERS TO HIS BROTHER THEO

WITHIN THE NATURAL TONES, the color brown traditionally creates atmospheres that evoke warmth and cosiness. Its many hues are gentle and silent, while its wide range of shades, including the deep or muted tones of orange, yellow, red and violet, produce a remarkable selection of different colors. Such brown tonalities offer us shades of beige, terracotta, raw and burnt umber, khaki, chocolate, taupe, maple, rust, ochre, warm sienna, honey and amber. The ability of brown to evoke warmth makes it an ideal foil for strong, exotic and vibrant colors. Browns are often used to offset the stronger, more dominant colors of turquoise, shocking pink, mauve, orange or lime green. Although brown can be used to tone down strong reds, blues or greens, such highly saturated primary colors tend to overwhelm its subtle earthiness.

Harmonious combinations using browns create effects that are nostalgic and romantic, feelings reminiscent of natural space and tranquillity, of comfort and contentment. Traditionally a color of calmness and passivity, brown is as dependable and changeable as the seasons. The color of earth, with its ploughed land and rich soil, brown also evokes autumn's brilliance followed by melancholy as leaves turn yellow and die.

In religious sects, brown indicates renunciation of all earthly things, the poverty and penitence of monasticism witnessed by the monk's brown habit, the return to the bare simplicity of the earth. As a symbol of humility and modesty connected to the soil, brown evokes sensations that are natural and genuine, feelings of being connected to the earth, to foundations that are grounding.

While brown belongs to the earth and is warm and secure, grey is cool and evasive, relating to clouds and mist. Although it, too, hints of asceticism and surrender, grey is as vague as the mist, recalling the concealment of clouds and all that evaporates. Its coolness distances emotions, disguises deep feelings, prefers what is gracious and remote. As a color of subdued instincts, evoking restrained elegance and purity, grey vibrations change only when other tonalities, such as mauve or pink, bring warmth to its essential coldness. Within the security of its delicacy and simplicity, grey brings feelings of distance and restraint as well as a sense of serenity and sophistication.

The variations of grey are cool and elegant, primarily consisting of equal proportions of white and black, varying according to whatever other color tones have been added. The grey area is between all colors, between the worlds, and greys exist in every part of the color wheel. There are hundreds of variations within grey – from warm greys with hints of pink or heather, to cool icy blue greys, to greeny greys – all defying description as they change throughout the day. With its strong similarity to brown, grey acts as a foil, blending easily with other soft, pastel colors. Whether pale dove grey or smoky blue grey, the effect is refined and sophisticated but always contained and careful.

AMBROSIA

The vast shades of different greys extend from complex combinations of warm brown, green or pink tones, through to cooler greys based on mixtures of black and white. In the latter, the tones of grey are cool and sophisticated, recalling the simplicity and harmony of classical design. Such greys evoke a rich harmony when coupled with the delicate shades of corals and lilacs, creating a gentle quality.

Grey is the only color for which there is no after image. The color of fantasies and dreaming, it suggests the total mist without any visibility. As if caught in a fog, only the naked truth can change the situation. Here emotion has turned into the grey coolness of distance, the color of separation from reality. In this design, it is the introduction of the warm coral tones and the sympathy of deep lilac shades that balances this cool, distant feeling. As grey also represents the beginning of a transformation, the sparkling beads suggest such an awakening, a brilliance that inspires and attracts one's eye.

Ambrosia, the fabled food and drink of the immortals, belongs to the dreamworld. The symmetry of this bargello pattern suggests that a core of stability is needed to attend both worlds, that myth and reality belong together, one being a mirror reflection of the other.

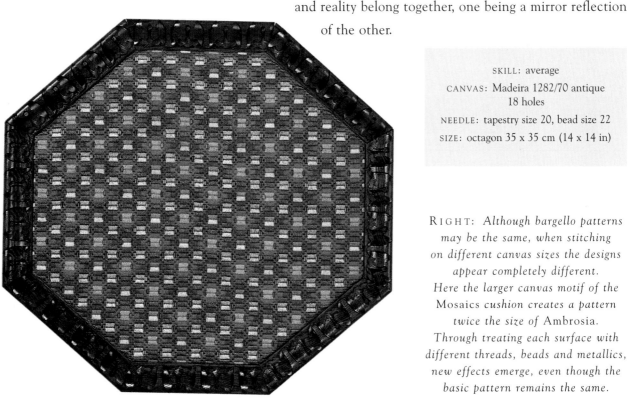

SKILL: average
CANVAS: Madeira 1282/70 antique
18 holes
NEEDLE: tapestry size 20, bead size 22
SIZE: octagon 35 x 35 cm (14 x 14 in)

RIGHT: *Although bargello patterns may be the same, when stitching on different canvas sizes the designs appear completely different. Here the larger canvas motif of the* Mosaics *cushion creates a pattern twice the size of Ambrosia. Through treating each surface with different threads, beads and metallics, new effects emerge, even though the basic pattern remains the same.*

Yarn Quantities

Madeira Cotton		*Metres*
light mauve	0807	20
med mauve	0806	20
deep mauve	2614	70
light brown	2601	20
rose brown	2310	20
med brown	2311	70

Madeira Decora		
light grey	1412	35
med grey	1440	30
dark grey	1441	140

copper, lilac and silver glass
bugle beads

CANVAS

◆ Cut the canvas, allowing a border of 5 cm (2 in) and bind the edges – *see Canvas, page 138*.
◆ Outline the design with a waterproof indelible marker, then draw central horizontal and vertical linesto mark the design's center.
◆ Spray paint the canvas brown – *see page 138*.

FOLLOWING THE CHART

◆ The chart shows the basic pattern and should be repeated as many times as necessary. This pattern can be adjusted to any size or shape.
◆ Stitch a complete row of dark grey motifs at the top or bottom, from right to left, beginning at its center, until finished in both directions. Stitch the next row of motifs, alternating colors. Continue until the pattern is completed.

STITCHING

◆ For instructions, *see Stitching, page 138*. To apply the glass beads, *see Beading, page 139*.
◆ Use Madeira 6 Stranded Cotton and Madeira Decora doubled. For a different effect this design can be stitched with a single thread.

MAKING THE TRAY

◆ Ask a carpenter to make the frame and insert the canvas – *see Suppliers, page 141*.

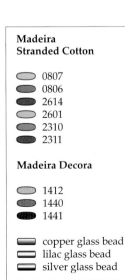

**Madeira
Stranded Cotton**

- 0807
- 0806
- 2614
- 2601
- 2310
- 2311

Madeira Decora

- 1412
- 1440
- 1441

- copper glass bead
- lilac glass bead
- silver glass bead

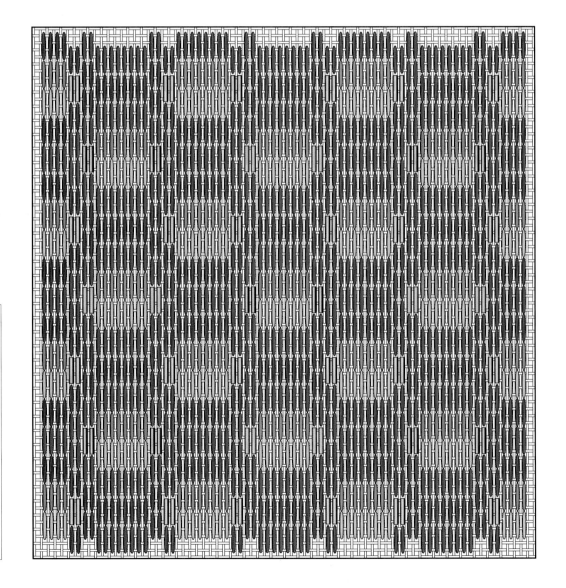

THISTLE

Rich brown tones evoke the scent of beautiful mahogany and rosewood, of autumn leaves and acres of planted fields. Their warmth invites one to stay, have a conversation, share a cup of tea. Sympathetic warm browns want to stay in the present time, be comfortable with traditional and unchangeable habits. Their sense of history couples with a willingness to let go of the past, to forgive and forget, to permit nature to take its course. Always aware of hours passing, this color vibration does not wish to waste time but prefers to enjoy the peace of the moment, the quintessence of the seasons, the natural rhythm of life. Its essence encourages informality and the sensitivity to respect instinctive feelings which belong to present time.

Vivid colors work well against its nourishing background. Here vibrant turquoise arouses the enthusiasm of creativity, encourages communication through artistic endeavors, provides the elasticity to remain flexible and open to new ideas. Turquoise, being close to lilac and deep violet, brings an awareness of cyclical rhythms, the sequences of the seasons, the sensitivity for suitable time planning and the talent for speaking softly while feeling deep understanding during change.

This traditional Florentine canvaswork uses heart-shaped motifs which alternate with small diamonds to create a bold pattern with an optical illusion. Its pattern is very easy to work once the first row has been established, with all subsequent rows following. Often called overlapping pomegranates, a change in the direction of the shading will greatly alter the overall effect.

SKILL: beginner
CANVAS: Madeira 1282/52 antique 13 holes
NEEDLE: tapestry size 18, bead size 22
SIZE: 41 x 39 cm (16 x 15½ in)

OVERLEAF: *This classic bargello pattern is extremely easy to stitch, yet the overall effect becomes quite dramatic through its striking use of color and its foil of creating a secondary pattern with deep, iridescent glass beads.*

Yarn Quantities

Madeira Cotton		Metres
turquoise	1203	65
deep green	1204	50
crimson	2609	65
mauve	0810	65
rust	0314	55
apricot	0311	60
purple	2714	65
deep lilac	2713	45

Needlepoint Border

turquoise	1203	10
deep green	1204	9
deep lilac	2713	10
crimson	2609	8
rust	0314	17
apricot	0311	6

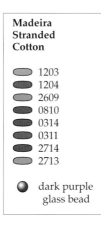

Madeira Stranded Cotton

- 1203
- 1204
- 2609
- 0810
- 0314
- 0311
- 2714
- 2713

- ● dark purple glass bead

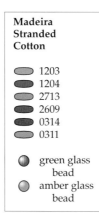

Madeira Stranded Cotton

- 1203
- 1204
- 2713
- 2609
- 0314
- 0311

- ● green glass bead
- ● amber glass bead

CANVAS

◆ Cut the canvas, allowing a border of 5 cm (2 in) and bind the edges – *see Canvas, page 138* for details.

◆ Outline the approximate size and shape of the design with a waterproof indelible marker, then draw central horizontal and vertical lines. The design's center is where these lines cross.

◆ Spray paint the canvas rust brown to unify any color showing through.

FOLLOWING THE CHART

◆ The motif below is the basic design and should be repeated as necessary to fill your canvas.

◆ Begin at the center of the canvas. Outline the central motif and continue outlining all the motifs to establish the overall pattern. Fill in the motifs using one color thread throughout. When completed, choose the next color and so on.

STITCHING

◆ For instructions, *see Stitching, page 138*. To apply the glass beads, *see Beading, page 139*.

◆ Use Madeira 6 Stranded Cotton as supplied.

MAKING THE CUSHION

◆ To complete this cushion, *see Finishing, page 139*.

HARMONY

There are taupe brown shades that lend depth and elegance wherever they are used, whose essence is relaxing, calming and understanding. Such subtle shades of brown radiate warmth, their spirit is welcoming and intimate, evoking the familiarity of history and family heirlooms. The depth of these brown tones brings a sense of continuity with the past. Here, combined with rich vermilion reds, the past is considered a cherished antique, evoking a sense of refinement and restfulness.

When combined with the strong subtlety of red, this nostalgic sense of tradition has an energy that stimulates the passions. Such remembrance is reflected in these designs whose time-honored bargello pattern complements antique footstools which are used today, the past and present joining. Here, the contentment of the past is provoked by the passion of red, emphasized by the elegance and refinement of metallic threads. Such copper threads symbolize the mystery of money as well as represent security against illness and psychic protection from negative interference.

The bargello pattern stitched for these footstools is the same pattern seen from different viewpoints, each design being a part of one another, hence the names *Harmony I and II*. These two patterns, alike yet different, juxtapose brown tonalities which are peaceful and unchangeable against red variations which are restless and agitated. These are opposites which complement each other while copper, which contains brown and red, links them and accentuates their warmth and vibrancy.

SKILL: average/advanced
CANVAS: Madeira 1282/70 antique 18 holes
NEEDLE: tapestry size 20
SIZE: 25 x 25 cm (10 x 10 in);
border 5 cm (2 in)

OVERLEAF: *Bargello patterns offer the challenge to create an extension of the pattern itself. Here the same pattern is divided in half, with each footstool extending a different half. Its intriguing effect complements and contrasts, adding enticement to what is essentially a classic design. Copper threads emphasize the lines of its pattern, heightening their differences and accentuating their similarity.*

Harmony I
Yarn Quantities

Madeira Cotton		Metres
brown	2007	20
brown	2602	20
brown	2304	20
brown	2305	20
red	2501	20
red	2502	20
red	0314	10
red	0313	10
red	0401	20

Madeira Decora		
deep crimson	1435	50
deep brown	1574	40

Madeira Metallic		
copper	3027/9803	6

Border: 1435, 1574 Decora, 2502
Cotton, 3027/9803 copper metallic

CANVAS

◆ Cut the canvas, allowing a border of 5 cm (2 in). Bind the edges – *see Canvas, page 138.*

◆ Outline the shape of the design with a waterproof indelible ink marker, then draw central horizontal and vertical lines to make four equal squared sections. The design's center point is where these lines cross.

◆ Spray paint the canvas rust brown to unify any color showing through.

FOLLOWING THE CHART

◆ These designs radiate from the center point, requiring the bargello pattern to be stitched from the center outwards.

◆ The stitch chart shows a fraction more than one quarter of the basic design. For one footstool, it represents the lower left-hand corner. For the other footstool, it represents the lower right-hand corner. In each design this section needs to be repeated four times, each section changing its direction.

◆ Stitch the lower half first, then reverse the canvas to complete the upper half.

◆ This pattern can be enlarged or made smaller, providing its overall size is squared.

STITCHING

◆ For detailed stitching instructions, *see Stitching, page 138.*

◆ Use Madeira Decora and Madeira 6 Stranded Cotton as supplied. Use Madeira Metallic doubled.

MAKING THE FOOTSTOOLS

◆ This pattern was designed to fit a pair of Victorian footstools and the canvas was mounted by a upholsterer. Its size can be adjusted to fit any square footstool, with the recommendation that it is fitted by a professional upholsterer.

Harmony II
Yarn Quantities

Madeira Cotton		Metres
brown	2007	20
brown	2602	20
brown	2304	20
brown	2305	20
red	2501	20
red	2502	20
red	0314	20
red	0313	10
red	0401	20

Madeira Decora		
crimson	1435	50
deep brown	1574	40

Madeira Metallic		
copper	3027/9803	6

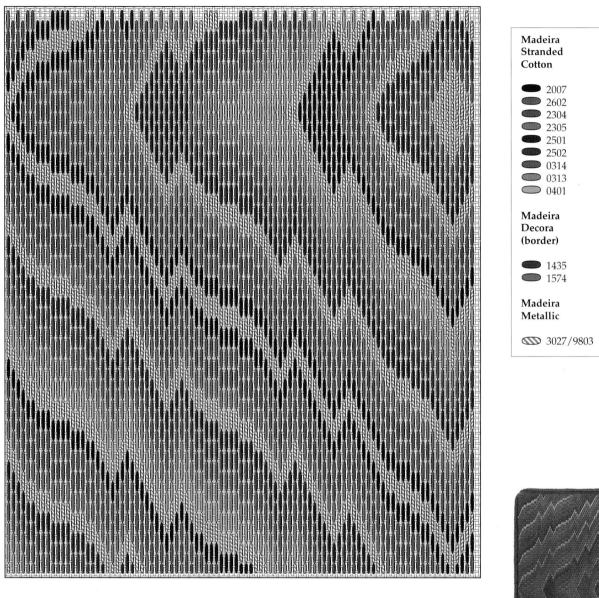

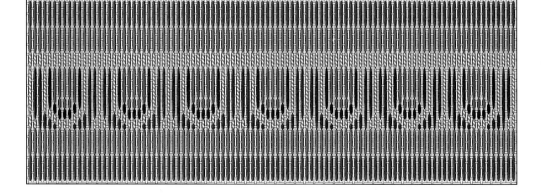

**Madeira
Stranded
Cotton**

2007
2602
2304
2305
2501
2502
0314
0313
0401

**Madeira
Decora
(border)**

1435
1574

**Madeira
Metallic**

3027/9803

GYPSY
CARPET BAG

Bargello is a celebration of pattern and color yet, more than anything else, color defines the character of the needlework. While each pattern has a distinct effect, color is the factor that blends them together. The *Gypsy Carpet Bag* expresses this relationship between pattern and color. Here, colors vary not only in intensity and hue, but also in degrees of warmth and coolness.

The ability of brown to reveal warmth as well as coolness makes it a superb foil against forceful, exotic and vibrant colors, hues that are otherwise difficult to match. It tones down a strong red, intense blue or deep green, adding solidity and presence. Against such a background of earth tones, the *Gypsy Carpet Bag* stimulates the desire to travel while keeping one's feet on the ground.

The color brown brings about a sense of nostalgia, clearing from the past, letting go of former burdens. The freeing of oneself from such attachments is the primary mood evoked by this bargello canvaswork, encouraging the freedom that comes with release. Its strong use of reds brings forth passion, deep pinks evoke the warmth of the heart, blues the serenity to move forwards, while deep yellows assure thoughtfulness in adventures to come.

In stitching the *Gypsy Carpet Bag* the unknown awakens, with the curiosity of what new travels will inspire, reflecting the emotions of brown that are open to change.

SKILL: average
CANVAS: Madeira 1282/60 antique, 15 holes
NEEDLE: tapestry size 18 or 20
SIZE: 46 x 50 x 7 cm (18 x 19½ x 2¾ in)

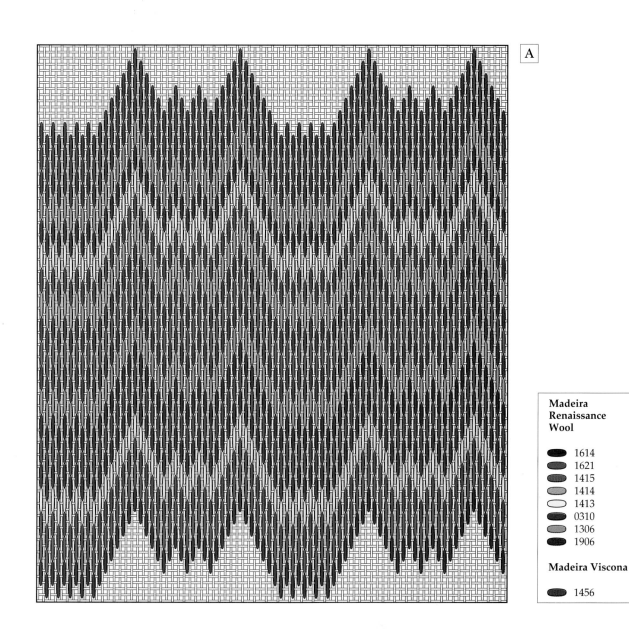

A

Madeira Renaissance Wool

- 1614
- 1621
- 1415
- 1414
- 1413
- 0310
- 1306
- 1906

Madeira Viscona

- 1456

LEFT: *A practical and challenging project, the Gypsy Carpet Bag travels well. Suitable for carrying canvases and threads, functional for taking on trips, this needlework design provides the luxury of attraction as well as the consideration of being sensible and useful. Its bargello pattern encourages the energy of movement through classical spires symbolizing the ups and downs of adventure, the desire to go forwards and discover all things unknown.*

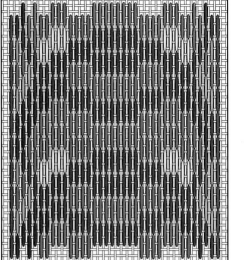

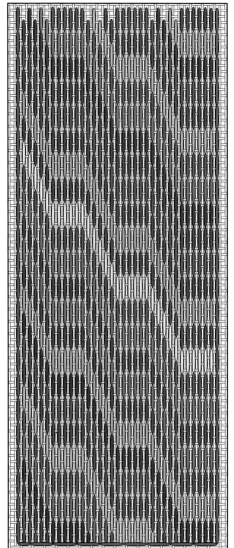

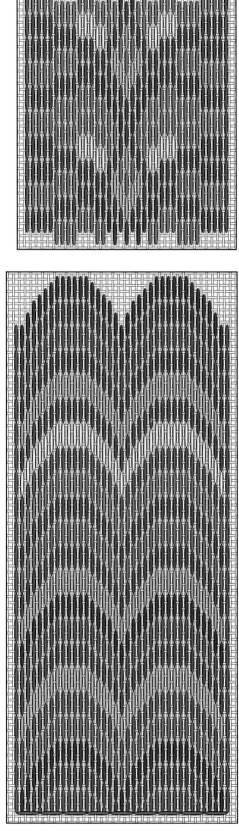

Yarn Quantities

Madeira Wool		Metres
deep green	1614	300
deep blue	1621	350
deep gold	1415	190
med gold	1414	160
light gold	1413	90
med red	0310	350
rose	1306	250
taupe brown	1906	700

Madeira Viscona		
brown	1456	475

CANVAS

◆ Cut the canvas, allowing a border of 5 cm (2 in). Bind the edges – *see Canvas, page 138.* The suggested height can easily be altered but to maintain the pattern, the width needs to be retained.

◆ Outline the shape of the design with a waterproof indelible marker, marking 2.5 cm (1 in) for the top pattern strip and 5 cm (2 in) for each of the four separate side pattern strips.

◆ Spray paint the canvas medium brown to unify any color showing through.

FOLLOWING THE CHART

◆ This design contains many traditional patterns. Its motifs are uncomplicated and, once the pattern is established, all subsequent rows follow clearly.

◆ The chart shows the basic design for this bag and should be repeated as necessary to complete the example stitched.

◆ Following the stitch chart work the center piece first, beginning at the bottom right-hand corner until each horizontal row of this section is complete.

◆ Finish the lower half of the stitching first, reversing the canvas to complete the upper half. Then complete all four border patterns one at a time, stitching from bottom to top. Stitch the border across the top of the design.

◆ On a separate strip of canvas, stitch the surrounding gusset.

◆ When stitching the bag, after the main section A is completed, the suggested stitching order is as follows:

    on the left side, stitch section C first, followed by section B

    on the right side, stitch section D first, followed by section E

    the surrounding gusset (section F) should be stitched separately, to be attached when the bag is sewn together

◆ The border design across the top of the bag is optional.

STITCHING

◆ For instructions, *see Stitching, page 138.*

◆ Use two strands of Madeira Renaissance Wool doubled. Use Madeira Viscona as supplied.

MAKING THE CARPET BAG

◆ For durability, strips of canvas have been placed inside the chenille fabric straps. The carpet bag itself is lined in taupe brown fabric.

◆ Unless skilled in making up, it is recommended that the *Gypsy Carpet Bag* is completed by a professional seamstress or upholsterer – *see Suppliers' addresses, page 141.*

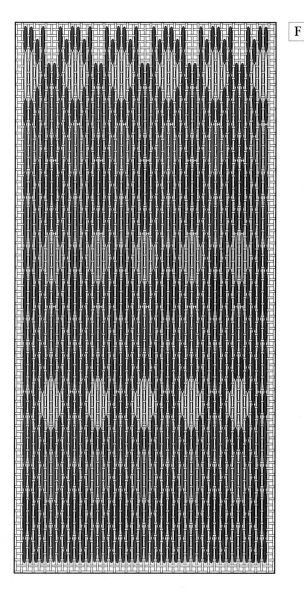

F

Y E L L O W

*W*ARM YELLOW, the color of supreme wisdom and quick intellect, was worshipped by the Greek sun god Apollo and held in high esteem by Minerva, the Greek goddess of wisdom. Honored by the god Mercury, the divine messenger between Heaven and Earth, its planet of the same name is closest to the sun. In ancient China, yellow symbolized nobility. Shining as the gold of the philosopher's stone, its radiance illuminated and imparted knowledge. Its brilliance sparkles as the yellow diamond and glistens as the yellow topaz.

YELLOW

*"But I mean to say that it is not easy to find a summer sun effect which is as
rich and as simple, and as pleasant to look at as the characteristics of
the other seasons. Spring is tender, green young corn and pink apple blossoms.
Autumn is the contrast of yellow leaves against violet tones.
Winter is the snow against black silhouettes. But now, if summer is the
opposition of blues against an element of orange, in the gold bronze of the corn,
one could paint a picture which expressed the mood of the seasons..."*

VINCENT VAN GOGH, LETTERS TO HIS BROTHER THEO

YELLOW IS THE HOTTEST, the most expansive and most burning of all the colors with an overflowing intensity. As the color of sunlight and cheerfulness, its warmth brings laughter, joy and delight. Its brightness returns the sparkle back to everyday life, its sunshine filling the atmosphere. Yellow has a cheerful spirit and an inner wisdom, making it a color beloved by writers, artists and creators.

Concerned with relationships, between both the environment and oneself, the yellow light of caution makes one think before acting. Linked with mental expansion and creative relaxation, this is an energizing color which brings vitality to spirit and thought.

Within any atmosphere its vibrations radiate feelings that are as warm and positive as the golden sun. Being the color of earthly wisdom, it is restless, always straining towards the pursuits of its ambitions. Yellow accelerates rapid thinking, hence governing the astrological sign Gemini. Its quick-witted and deeply intensive thoughts are concerned with bringing ideas into creation.

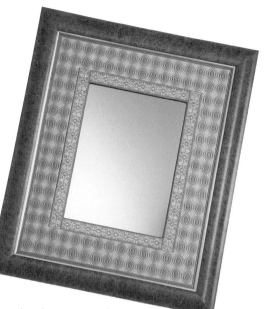

Due to its earthly connections, yellow belongs to the fertility of the soil and the fertility within marriage. In former times it was the color of marriage canopies, the wedding dress, the bride's veil, even bridal slippers. Its color symbolized peace and purity of spirit and the constancy of faith, bringing with it the union of wisdom and fortune, the richness and power of gold. Because of its emotional content, yellow is concerned with nourishment and assimilation, representing the whole nervous and digestive system. As it increases the rate of metabolism, so its healing process cleanses, stimulates and organizes the nervous system. Its warm vibrations calm anxiety and irrational fears, relaxing tensions so that one can absorb and integrate with the world around.

In an interior environment, yellow brings people together, emphasizing the union of love and wisdom. Through its powers of reason and the awareness of clear thinking, yellow helps to encourage everyday happiness and feelings of satisfaction within oneself and with others. Its cheerfulness inspires one to achieve new works with confidence and optimism. Yellow is the color of life and light which attracts to individuals the things they most desire. Being the masculine side which traditionally asserts what one needs and wants, its brightness draws energy towards itself. Through integrating the sun's golden rays, the color yellow brings dignity and recognition, as well as peace and purity of spirit, into one's life.

REFLECTIONS

Yellow, a brilliant color that is light and optimistic, fills a room with the sun's luminosity. Here created as a bargello mirror frame, *Reflections* combines silks, gold metallics and shimmering Decora threads in shades which enhance an environment with their rich elegance. As an intellectual color, yellow is ideal for rooms where conversation and thinking processes take place, encouraging mental expansion and helping one to reach intelligent decisions and express clear ideas.

Because of its lightness and feeling of luxury, yellow brings pleasure and joy to both creativity and communication. It transforms ideas into concrete form and welcomes the intake of new information. Through its warmth one relaxes and becomes inspired in undertaking challenging projects. Its vibrations help to overcome idleness, expand thoughts and stimulate the imagination.

The energy of yellow brings forth resourcefulness, clarity and innovative ideas. It clears emotional confusion, encourages freedom from fear and assists in letting go of illusions. Being free from feelings of limitations, its radiant vibrations enhance confidence in thought and speech. The calmness yet intensity of yellow uplifts personal creative thoughts, as well as brings pleasure in conversation.

In the design *Reflections*, the yellow tonalities have the warmth of ochre, the radiance of gold threads, the feelings of serenity and vibrancy together. The reinterpretation of this classic pattern results in elegance and simplicity, enhanced by the subtlety of its bronze mirror.

SKILL: average/advanced
CANVAS: Madeira 1282/70 antique 18 holes
NEEDLE: tapestry size 20
SIZE: 57 x 47 cm (22½ x 18½ in)

RIGHT: *Elegant and refined, appreciating the aesthetics of candlelight and evening fires, this design encourages reflection, creating a mood that is romantic and yet real. Its feminine needlepoint border harmonizes well with its formal masculine pattern. Luxurious silk threads contrast with the beauty of natural grained wood, creating an effect that is both extravagant and earthbound.*

Yarn Quantities

Madeira Silk		Metres
deep gold	2211	75
med gold	2213	65
light yellow	0105	45
Madeira Decora		
med gold	1571	115
light gold	1525	70
Madeira Metallic		
gold	9803/3008	20

CANVAS

◆ Cut the canvas, allowing a border of 5 cm (2 in) all round. Bind the edges – *see Canvas, page 138* for details.
◆ Outline the approximate size and shape of the design with a tested, waterproof indelible ink marker, including the center border design.
◆ Spray paint the canvas ochre (deep yellow) to unify any color showing through.

FOLLOWING THE CHART

◆ Once established, this intricate bargello pattern is uncomplicated but needs close attention to follow its basic lines.
◆ The stitch chart shows the basic design for this wall mirror and should be repeated as many times as necessary to complete the example stitched. This pattern can be adjusted to any size or shape desired.
◆ Begin stitching from the base upwards, first establishing the half diamond pattern, then stitching the complete row. Work one color at a time, completing each row in sequence.
◆ The center border design should be stitched last, after the outside frame pattern has been completed.

STITCHING

◆ For instructions, *see Stitching, page 138*.
◆ Use Madeira Metallic doubled. Use Madeira Silk and Madeira Decora as supplied.

MAKING THE WALL MIRROR

◆ Here smoked glass has been selected for the mirror. It is advisable to have the bargello pattern mounted on cardboard and framed by a framer who is familiar with handling canvas or textiles – *see Suppliers' Addresses, page 141*.

Madeira Silk

2211
2213
0105

Madeira Decora

1571
1525

Madeira Metallic

9803/3008

RUSSIAN MUSIC

Russian Music is a splendid example of the yellow tones which form the base of other colors, namely rust, copper, burnt siena and olive green, while ochre yellow contains red tints. These warm colors, which are based on the yellow, orange and red parts of the spectrum, feel approachable and

immediate, the greater their intensity the more they project forward. These sympathetic colors give back light and so are active, advancing and intense. The effects they produce create bargello patterns which are dramatic and dynamic. Here this complex color combination shows how imaginative designs can be enhanced by using innovative threads which blend together.

Reminding us of the dramatic intensity and bravura of Russian music, this design flows with a tonal resonance. It holds the luxury and richness of melodramatic chords, the passionate drama of symphonies by Tchaikovsky, Rimsky-Korsakov, Stravinsky. Its enthusiasm enriches a room through its bold interplay of colors. Such inspiring effects vibrate as musical chords, generating color excitement. The use of luxurious silk threads complements such emotions, leaving one with feelings sumptuous and expansive.

Russian Music brings profound passion and elegance into an environment whether spacious or intimate. Its vibrations come from the heart and connect with intense emotions. It stimulates pleasure and appreciates the results of creative endeavors which appeal to both masculine and feminine energies.

SKILL: average
CANVAS: Madeira 1282/52 antique 13 holes
NEEDLE: tapestry size 18 or 20
SIZE: 41 x 92 cm (16¼ x 36¼ in)

OVERLEAF: *With an abundant use of romantic colors for a dramatic effect, this seat cushion evokes feelings of delight and exuberance as its undulating rhythms cascade across its surface.*
Such large scale repetition of a pattern represents the way bargello designs were used for centuries to cover large surfaces as its stitches were quick to work and results immediately satisfying.

Yarn Quantities

Madeira Silk		Metres
gold	2211	155
rust	0401	125
rust	0402	150
brown	2114	175
red	0511	210
rust	0811	95
black	black	195

Madeira Metallic Glamour		
black	2470	37

CANVAS

◆ Cut the canvas to the desired size, allowing a border of 5 cm (2 in) all around for finishing.

◆ Tape or stitch all four sides to prevent fraying, *see Canvas, page 138* for details.

◆ Outline the approximate size and shape of the design with a tested, waterproof indelible ink marker, allowing for the border design.

◆ Using an ochre (yellow brown) fast-drying spray enamel paint, spray across the canvas surface to unify any color showing through.

FOLLOWING THE CHART

◆ This design is not difficult but requires careful attention in counting the canvas threads, a necessity in mastering the Hungarian point stitch.

◆ The stitch chart shows the basic design for this seat cushion and should be repeated as many times as necessary to complete the example stitched. This pattern can be adjusted to any size or shape desired.

◆ The bottom right-hand section of the border should be stitched first with a mitred corner (*see Stitching, page 138*), then the inside pattern stitched next. This single motif design is then completed one row at a time, starting within the established corner border, working from right to left until each horizontal row is completed.

◆ After finishing the lower half of the stitching first, reverse the canvas to complete the upper half of the design, taking care that the mitred corner border meets. When the center pattern and the surrounding border have been completed, outline the border sections in black metallic thread.

STITCHING

◆ For instructions, *see Stitching, page 138*.

◆ Use one thread of Madeira Metallic doubled. Use Madeira Silk doubled.

MAKING THE SEAT CUSHION

◆ To complete this seat cushion, *see Finishing instructions for a cushion, page 139*.

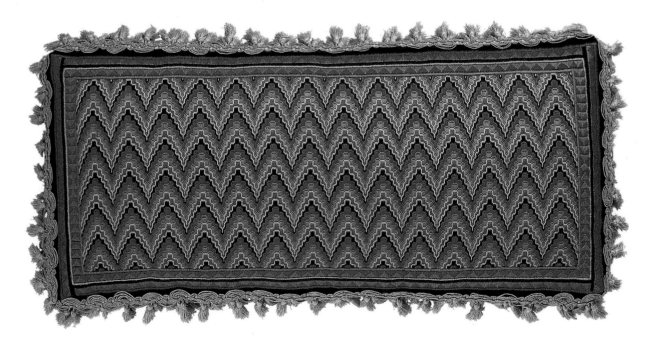

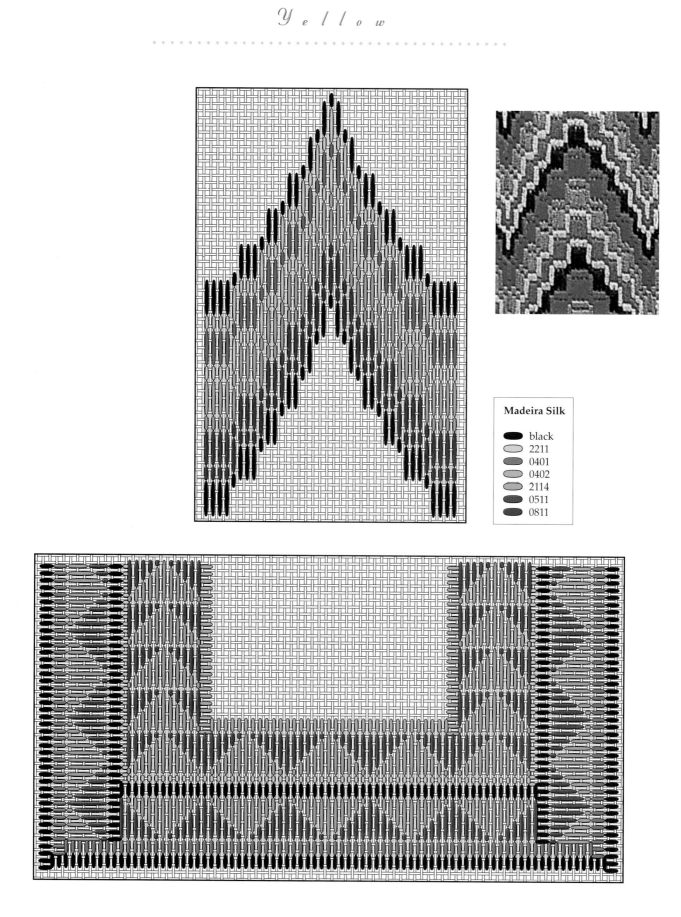

Madeira Silk

- black
- 2211
- 0401
- 0402
- 2114
- 0511
- 0811

EXOTICA

When used as the main color, warm ochre yellow conveys an atmosphere of cosiness. Particularly favorable in rooms without sun, the depth and opulence of *Exotica* adds lustre to colorless days. Warm yellows recall summer sunflowers, the deep intensity of a topaz jewel, profound feelings of contentment with elegance. These colors bring light into all aspects of one's personality and help to connect with inner wisdom.

Yellows look clearest when combined with browns and here warm ochre is shadowed by metallic copper threads, coupled with shimmering amber beads. Complementing the pale buttery tones against the cooler shade of lavender lends a mellow warmth, undemanding and restful to the eye. As its deeper yellow becomes rich amber, a gentle golden hue with a hint of red brings about serenity. Here one finds joy in simplicity, bringing warmth and freshness into an environment. Undisturbed by obstacles, these soothing colors reflect ease and lightness in trials and difficulties.

Exotica is comfortable where space is intimate and conducive to restful moments. Here intense ochre and rust feel as sunrise and sunset, a combination that enjoys relaxation and leisure. Its essence radiates emotions of sensuous joy as one experiences tranquillity and serenity. Appealing to one's private self, these colors stimulate thoughts concerning relationships with another or with others.

SKILL: average
CANVAS: Madeira 1282/60 antique 15 holes
NEEDLE: tapestry size 20, bead size 22
SIZE: 46 x 51 cm (18 x 20 in)

Resting on such a bolster encourages contemplation to find security and profound pleasure with oneself and in communication with others.

OVERLEAF: *Contentment and containment are the themes of this bargello pattern, the harmony of the self and the shadow. Its diamond patterns speak of richness, the wealth within oneself that encourages a time to rest and think, the appreciation of quiet time alone. Tones of ochre and amber respect such wisdom, the lavender being the scent of tranquillity and the amber beads the sparkle within.*

Yarn Quantities

Madeira Cotton		Metres
deep rust	2306	20
rust	2302	70
deep gold	2010	80
light gold	2011	70
mauve	2613	180
Madeira Decora		
rust	1574	110
Madeira Metallic Lame		
copper	9814/427	140
Madeira Viscona		
rust	1558	28

CANVAS

◆ Cut the canvas and bind the edges – *see page 138*.
◆ Outline the design with a waterproof indelible marker. Spray paint the canvas ochre (yellow brown).

FOLLOWING THE CHART

◆ The stitch chart shows the basic design and should be repeated as necessary.
◆ Begin in the bottom right-hand corner and establish the half diamond pattern. Then stitch the metallic thread and outline the entire diamond pattern, stitching one row at a time, from right to left when the center pattern is finished, stitch the side borders in vertical order of color.

STITCHING

◆ For instructions, *see Stitching, page 138*.
◆ Use Madeira Metallic Lame, Madeira 6 Stranded Cotton and Madeira Decora doubled. Use Madiera Viscona as supplied.

Madeira Stranded Cotton

- 2306
- 2302
- 2010
- 2011
- 2613

Madeira Decora

- 1574

Madeira Lame Metallic

- 9814/427

Madeira Viscona

- 1558
- amber glass bead

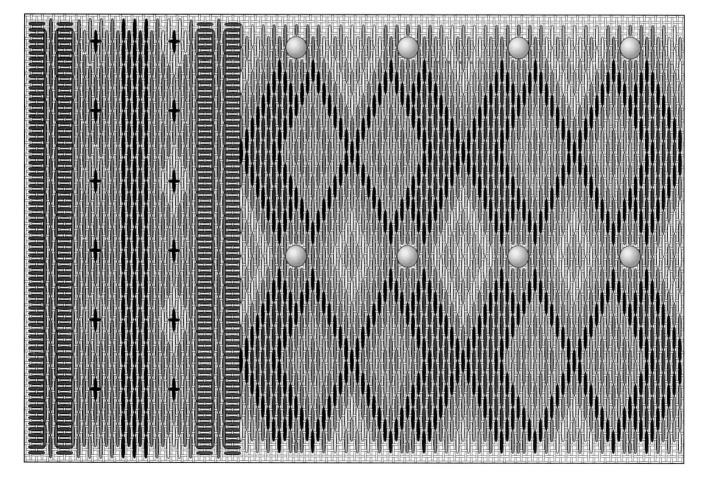

ITALIA

A bargello design inspired by its complementary fabric, *Italia* creates a luminous and warm effect through its luxurious combination of the gold lustre of Decora threads coupled with exotic colors. Its deep golden tones combine effectively with the rich colors of darker reds, sea greens, soft turquoise, violet and purple. This sensitive juxtaposition of colors creates a unique pattern as feminine and alluring as the mystery of the East.

Here the splendor of gold tempts and attracts, entices one to realms ruled by the imagination. Its color nuances allow hidden wisdom to dance with the mystery of intuition and encourage the interplay of deep gold, violet and purple to create an effect that is timeless and magical.

Such golden tones open the pathway to vision, suggest knowledge from past times. They intimate the sensitivity that to know is more valuable than to possess. This design honors the dreamer who has the instinctive courage to fulfil deep aspirations, reminiscent of the golden sun reflecting the intuitive moon. Appealing to a charismatic personality, here one seeks the depth below the surface, enjoys bringing the unknown into present life, creates a magical space with a clear vision of the future.

The colors of *Italia* are well suited for personal rooms where one wishes to feel luxurious and exotic, dream and explore realms of the imagination, contemplate creative endeavors. The vibrations of *Italia* encourage private time for one's own thoughts and musings.

SKILL: average
CANVAS: Madeira 1282/56 antique 14 holes
NEEDLE: tapestry size 18 or 20
SIZE: 30 x 63 cm (11¾ x 25 in)

RIGHT: *The colors and motifs of* Italia, *inspired by its companion fabric, create bargello patterns that harmonize while being different. One cushion design, using traditional curves and spires, reverses its image at the center point, its needlepoint border motivated by the fabric itself. The second* Italia *design carries this mirror reflection throughout with the addition of a decorative border and lavish trim.*

Yarn Quantities

Madeira Cotton		Metres
med green	1704	40
dark green	1204	48
mauve	2613	20
mauve	0805	80
purple	0714	48
rust	0811	48
crimson	0602	48
green	1703	20
brown	2009	52
Madeira Decora		
burgundy	1435	39
gold	1425	79

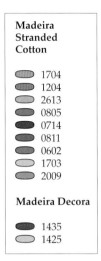

Madeira Stranded Cotton	
	1704
	1204
	2613
	0805
	0714
	0811
	0602
	1703
	2009
Madeira Decora	
	1435
	1425

CANVAS

◆ Cut the canvas to the desired size, allowing a border of 5 cm (2 in) all around for finishing.

◆ Tape or stitch all four sides to prevent fraying, *see Canvas, page 138* for details.

◆ Outline the approximate size and shape of the design with a tested, waterproof indelible ink marker, allowing for the border pattern. Then draw horizontal and vertical lines. The design's center point is where these lines cross.

◆ Using a blue fast-drying spray enamel paint, spray across the canvas surface to unify any color showing through.

FOLLOWING THE CHART

◆ This imaginative design looks complicated but is based on a traditional single row pattern which then mirrors itself, all subsequent rows merely following.

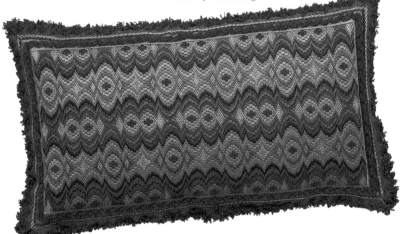

◆ The stitch chart shows the basic design for this cushion and should be repeated as many times as necessary to complete the example stitched. This pattern can be adjusted to any size or shape desired.

◆ The top right-hand section with the border first should be stitched with a mitred corner (*see Stitching, page 138*), then the inside pattern stitched next. This single motif design is then completed one row at a time, starting within the established corner border, working from right to left until each horizontal row is completed.

◆ After finishing the upper half of the stitching first, reverse the canvas to complete the lower half, once again taking care that the mitred corner border meets.

STITCHING

◆ For instructions, *see Stitching, page 138*.

◆ Use Madeira Decora and Madeira 6 Stranded Cotton doubled.

MAKING THE CUSHION

◆ To complete this bargello cushion, *see Finishing, page 139*.

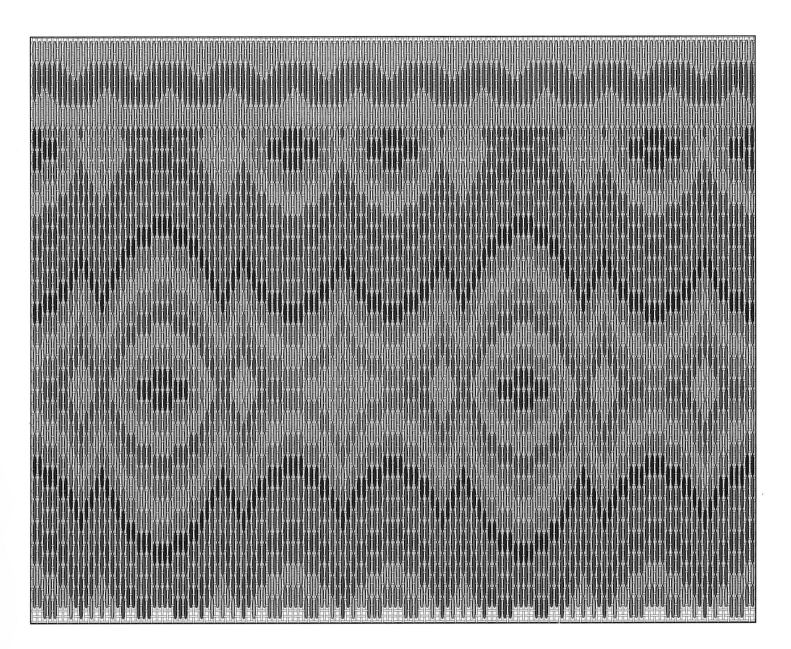

R E D

As a MASCULINE SYMBOL of power, red was the color of emperors, generals and the nobility. In antiquity there was a widely held belief that red protected one from dangers. As a feminine symbol, red represented the mother goddess of India, associated with the principle of creation. It was considered the marriage color of India, the Chinese color of luck and happiness. As an agitating, heat-giving color, red belongs to the planet Mars, the Sun and the astrological sign Taurus.

RED

"But if only you had been with us on Sunday,
when we saw a red vineyard, all red like red wine. In the distance it
turned to yellow, and then a green sky with the sun,
the earth after the rain violet, sparkling yellow here and there
where it caught the reflection of the setting sun."

VINCENT VAN GOGH, LETTERS TO HIS BROTHER THEO

*R*ED IS A CURIOUS COLOR with both cool and warm aspects, a masculine and feminine side, attracting the passions of both war and love. Its masculine warrior energy thrives on conquest and control, willpower and strength, seduction and irresistible lust. Its male extrovert qualities belong to the bright red shades which are dazzling and fiery, asserting endurance and physical strength, stimulating physical activity and vital energy. Such ambitious tones bring about action, all that is bold and brave, creating an environment that generates both activity and vitality.

While all shades of red stimulate the heart, flame passions and create excitement, its feminine side belongs to the deep, dark shades of crimson, scarlet, magenta and burgundy. These colors are secretive and nocturnal and hold within them the feminine mystery of life. They create an atmosphere of warmth and subtle excitement, the rich sensuality of seduction, the deep romantic red roses of passionate love with their luxurious hidden desires. Here 'the fires that burn within' arouse and quicken magnetic attraction, evoke feelings of willingness to love even under difficult conditions. The color red gives its best in relationships, helps to overcome resentments and anger, recognizes and fulfils one's heart's desires.

Evoking strong emotions, whether from passions of love or passions of war, red energy seeks victory and success, requiring courage and devotion. Vital and intense, its essence brings forth a strong statement, its vividness requires awareness of present time. As one of the strongest colors in the spectrum, red's boldness appears to advance towards one, furthering an atmosphere of assertion and calling attention to oneself.

Concerned with feelings of psychological and physical well-being, red's strongest connection is to the heart center. Although it gives the greatest energy of all the colors, surprisingly red has the slowest rate of vibration, thus increasing circulation and bringing security and stability to the physical body. Traditionally its allegorical stone, the ruby, was believed to bring the bearer good health and protection from disease.

Connected to the basic emotions of love, passion and virility, red affects the physical body and psychological self-confidence. Its most positive aspect brings warmth and stability, incredible joy towards life, learning to love in all situations. Its moods shift when mixed with other base colors, varying from soft pink to rose, from cherry red to strawberry, from cranberry to mulberry. Such colors promise new beginnings and new life. Cool reds are those that have blue in them, such as crimson, raspberry, cerise, pink and purple. These tones bring compassion after passion is spent, soothing unspoken frustrations and resentment. Yet no matter what the shade, red remains an emotional color evoking strong responses.

STAINED GLASS

Stained Glass, inspired by sunlight reflected through luminous colored glass, is coupled with classic bargello repetitive patterns. Here the predominant color red is accented against its complementary colors of yellow and blue, while its green tones result from combining yellow and blue. Such a complex yet harmonious design appeals to those with courage and heart who dare to push forward into the unknown, individuals who feel empowered to act rather than react.

The nine emblems represent a significant number. Nine symbolizes completion and fulfilment, the beginning and end, the harmonious coming together of male and female energies. Here the red passion of fire projects from the waters of emotion, its blue-green background interspersed with the gold of richness and spirituality. Through mixing five different threads, an allegory evolves based on saying 'yes' to life, connecting and extending with joy, freeing from old, limiting patterns.

Expansion and excitement are the keynotes of *Stained Glass*, the infectious enthusiasm for life, expressing communication on all levels, stimulating creative and passionate feelings. Here, through vibrations that are decisive and assertive, each color transforms ideas into action, gives warmth, support and attention to one another.

SKILL: advanced
CANVAS: Madeira 1282/60 antique 15 holes
NEEDLE: tapestry size 18 or 20, bead size 22
SIZE: 46 x 46 cm (18 x 18 in)

RIGHT: *Stimulated by the abundance of patterns available from the past, Stained Glass became a design that created itself. One stitch led to the next, the large central motifs resulting from small interlocking diamonds, the gold threads accentuating the rhythms that emerged, with the inspiration for the glass red beads coming last, yet another extension that enhanced this pattern.*

Yarn Quantities

Madeira Wool

light green	1619	25
med green	1613	25
dark green	1505	50
light blue	1004	50
med blue	1006	25
med red	0207	50
deep red	1101	50
crimson	0209	25

CANVAS

◆ Cut the canvas, allowing a border of 5 cm (2 in). Bind the edges – *see Canvas, page 138.*

◆ Outline the design with a waterproof indelible marker, then draw central horizontal and vertical lines to mark the design's center.

◆ Spray paint the canvas red.

FOLLOWING THE CHART

◆ The chart shows the basic design and should be repeated as necessary.

◆ Following the design's center point, begin by stitching the central motif (of which there are nine repeats), leaving the red glass beads until last. Then stitch the four small diamond shapes around this center motif, continuing to stitch the repetitive top and bottom diamonds establish the main pattern. Follow the chart to continue this repeated pattern and observe the finished cushion to see its precise placement.

STITCHING

◆ For instructions, *see Stitching, page 138.* For *Beading, see page 139.*

◆ Use Madeira Metallic and Madeira Decora doubled. Use two strands of Madeira Renaissance Wool doubled.

MAKING THE CUSHION

◆ To complete, *see Finishing, page 139.*

Yarn Quantities

Madeira Decora		*Metres*
brown	1456	150
red	1439	75
Madeira Metallic		
gold	9810/325	165

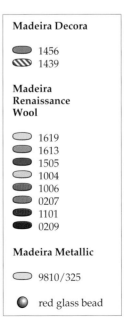

Madeira Decora

- 1456
- 1439

Madeira Renaissance Wool

- 1619
- 1613
- 1505
- 1004
- 1006
- 0207
- 1101
- 0209

Madeira Metallic

- 9810/325
- ● red glass bead

LATTICE

The covered red brick *Lattice* works well as a doorstop, a bookend, a surface to rest objects upon. This intriguing color combination, exceedingly vibrant and intense, has both cool and warm aspects. Its red-orange is soothing yet strong and bright. Its other shades are cool rich reds, all with blue in them, including raspberry, cherry and crimson while its violet accent calms the intensity of these other colors.

This combination brings emotional energy to an environment where one needs clarity of thought for it helps to clear confusion from the mind. Its vibrations are positive and passionate, encouraging freedom in thinking while stimulating physical strength to undertake new things.

Such a brilliant red energy transforms feelings on a psychological, emotional and physical level. The dynamic quality of these reds enhances productivity and renews ambition. The interspersed touches of violet release negativity, cool and calm hidden emotions, encouraging a sense of distance so impulsive reactions can be changed into meaningful actions.

Wherever it is placed, *Lattice* brings the continual enjoyment of a small object which makes a strong statement. Its color combination enriches the environment, its design integrates a traditional bargello pattern with an intricate border motif whose colorful effect accentuates the vibrant emotions of passion and productivity.

SKILL: average
CANVAS: Madeira 1282/70 antique 18 holes
NEEDLE: tapestry size 20
SIZE: 7 x 11.5 x 22 cm (2¾ x 4½ x 9 in)

OVERLEAF: *A brick doorstop wants to be more than just useful – it asks to be an object of beauty, something fanciful and unforgettable. This pattern extended itself through experimenting with various colored threads, resulting in the surprise of distinctively different effects created from using the same bargello pattern in different color combinations.*

R e d

· ·

Yarn Quantities

Madeira Cotton		Metres
aubergine	2609	20
crimson	0602	20
dark pink	0705	30
deep lilac	0706	20
dusty pink	0604	20
red	0510	30
deep red	0508	30
deep red	0511	30
dark red	0513	30

CANVAS

◆ Cut the canvas with the border design, plus an extra border of 5 cm (2 in). Bind the edges.

◆ Outline the brick's shape; draw horizontal and vertical lines to mark the design's center.

◆ Spray paint the canvas red.

FOLLOWING THE CHART

◆ Repeat the design on the chart as needed.

◆ Thread needles with the complete color sequence for the interlocking sections, i.e. four red shades graded from light to dark.

◆ From the center, work outwards, stitching all four colors to establish a four-row sequence.

STITCHING

◆ For instructions, *see Stitching, page 138.*

◆ Use Madeira 6 Stranded Cotton as supplied.

MAKING THE RED BRICK

◆ *See Finishing instructions, page 139.* Then cover the brick with polyester stuffing to even the surface. After the canvas is sewn together, slip-stitch some felt to the brick's underside.

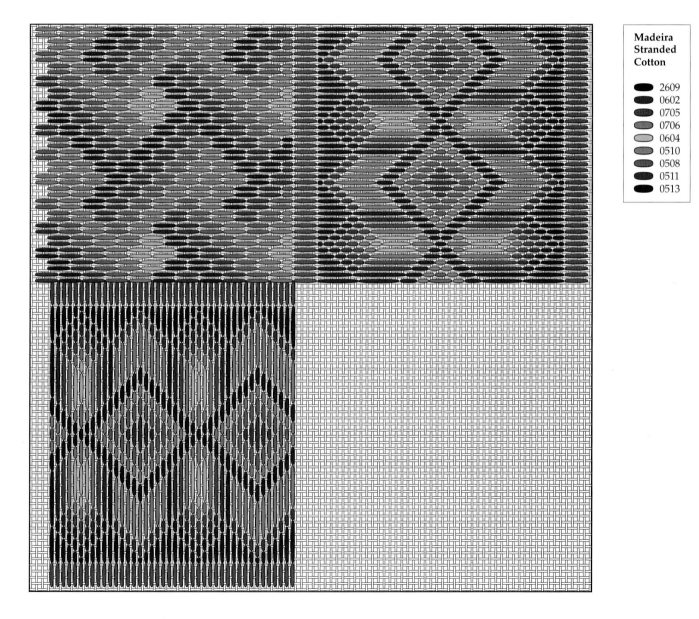

**Madeira
Stranded
Cotton**

- 2609
- 0602
- 0705
- 0706
- 0604
- 0510
- 0508
- 0511
- 0513

PHOENIX

This design symbolizes the sacred Phoenix – the mythical bird of matchless splendor and longevity, which is consumed by fire and rises reborn from its own ashes. Its energy is one of regeneration and renewal, symbolized by the creative and destructive fire with its continual endings and beginnings.

In ancient China, the male Phoenix represented happiness, while the female was an emblem of the empress. Together they symbolized marital bliss. Here the warm background recalls the earth from which the fire burns, while the copper threads and beads symbolize the magic of the Phoenix.

The rich red colors within this bargello pattern represent abundant energy, including psychic energy, which magnetically draws others towards its vibration. Its vivid combination of reds brings deep peace and freshness into life. Just as the Phoenix represents the mystery and strength of the physical self, so its wonder brings happiness and good fortune to the home. The accents of warm coral red bring forth the love of self which enables one to receive love from others. As a color of wisdom, red connects love with deep personal joy and projects its inner beauty into the outer surroundings.

SKILL: average/advanced
CANVAS: Madeira 1282/70 antique 18 holes
NEEDLE: tapestry size 20, bead size 22
SIZE: 47 x 42 cm (18½ x 16½ in)

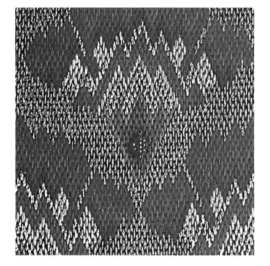

RIGHT: As Phoenix *was created for an antique firescreen, the bargello pattern selected was a traditional one with some special effects added. A classic carnation pattern was reinterpreted to represent the magical Phoenix bird, its thirteen motifs alluding to both the misfortune and magnificence of this fabled bird.*

Yarn Quantities

Madeira Cotton		Metres
red	0510	40
red	0508	18
coral	0512	15
orange	0214	20
apricot	0210	20
orange	0309	10
burnt orange	0312	13
Madeira Decora		
brown	1574	160
Madeira Wool		
crimson	0209	50
Madeira Metallic		
copper	3027/9803	50

CANVAS

◆ Cut the canvas to the desired size, allowing a border of 5 cm (2 in) all around for finishing.

◆ Tape or stitch all four edges to prevent fraying – *see Canvas, page 138* for details.

◆ Outline the approximate size and shape of the design with a tested, waterproof indelible ink marker. Then draw central and vertical lines. The design's center point is where these lines cross.

◆ Using a red fast-drying spray enamel paint, spray across the surface of the canvas to unify any color showing through.

FOLLOWING THE CHART

◆ This design is a variation of the historical Florentine flame pattern, also known as the carnation pattern. It is a series of zigzag and diamond shapes within a specific outline.

◆ The stitch chart shows the basic design for this firescreen and should be repeated as many times as necessary to complete the example stitched. This pattern can be adjusted to any size or shape desired, the border design shown on the chart being an optional suggestion.

◆ This single motif design is begun from the center point of the design and worked outwards. It is advisable to outline all the motifs desired first, then begin at the bottom and work upwards when filling in the background stitch. When stitching each outline motif, it is helpful to finish one color at a time throughout all the motifs, doing the same with each following color until the motifs are completed.

STITCHING

◆ For detailed stitching instructions, *see Stitching, page 138*.

◆ Use two strands of Madeira Renaissance Wool doubled. Use Madeira 6 Stranded Cotton as supplied. Use Madeira Metallic doubled.

MAKING THE FIRESCREEN

◆ This pattern was designed for an antique firescreen, mounted by an upholsterer. Its size can be adjusted to fit any firescreen, with the recommendation that it be fitted into the frame by a professional upholsterer.

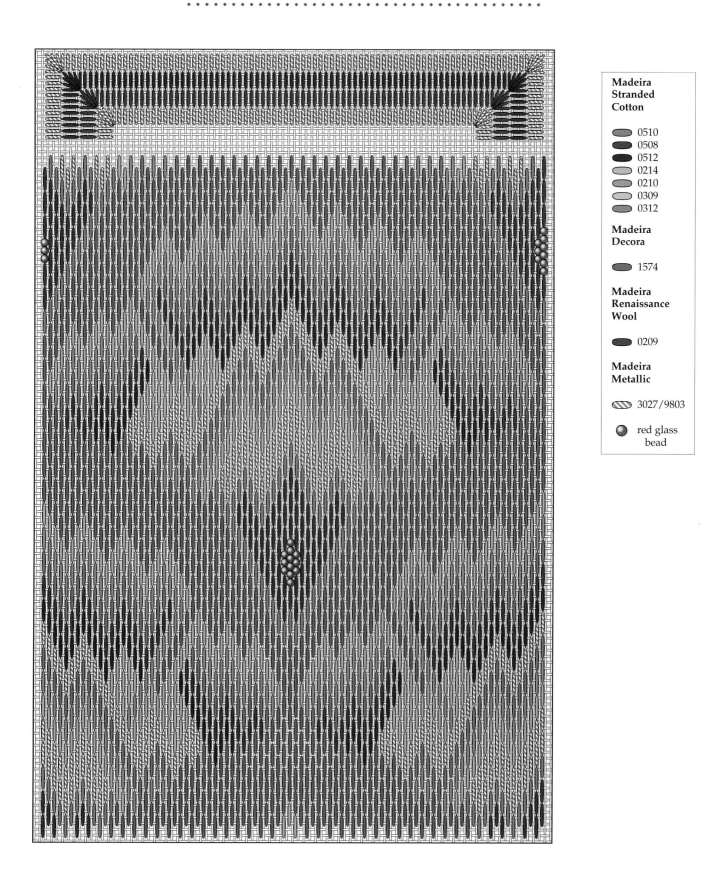

**Madeira
Stranded
Cotton**

0510
0508
0512
0214
0210
0309
0312

**Madeira
Decora**

1574

**Madeira
Renaissance
Wool**

0209

**Madeira
Metallic**

3027/9803

red glass
bead

RENAISSANCE

The design *Renaissance* is adapted from a fifteenth-century flame stitch pattern from Chastleton House in Gloucestershire, England where dressing room walls were covered with extensive canvaswork. Its flowing repetitive pattern of two different double images reflects the harmony of male/female energies.

This luxurious silk design, with its dominance of soft coral and deep reds, suggests the intimacy and passion of unconditional love coupled with warmth and compassion. Such shared love brings with it the deep inner joy of green and the radiant wisdom of gold. Between the many red tonalities, the blue and green sections symbolize tranquillity and spaciousness, thus allowing space for each person to develop individual identity.

Tieback
SKILL: average
CANVAS: Madeira 1282/70 antique 18 holes
NEEDLE: tapestry size 20, bead size 22
SIZE: 12.5 x 84 cm (5 x 33 in)

Pelmet
SKILL: average/advanced
CANVAS: Madeira 1282/70 antique 18 holes
NEEDLE: tapestry size 20
SIZE: 25 x 356 cm (10 in x 24 feet) – this is for three sides of a four-poster bed

RIGHT: *Whether befitting a four poster bed or drawing room curtains, bargello was traditionally favored for covering large surfaces, with satisfying results seen within a relatively short period of time. Not only did such stitching create feelings of luxury and extravagance, it aroused a sense of loyalty and devotion to the home by undertaking such extensive projects.*

Tieback
Yarn Quantities

Madeira Silk		Metres
deep mauve	0811	10
deep rust	0401	20
med rust	0402	12
dark green	1204	10
deep olive	1312	10
med olive	1407	20
med mauve	0812	10
apricot	0214	10
sapphire blue	1005	20
gold	2211	20
terracotta	2306	10

Madeira Decora		
deep rose	1434	10
burgundy	1435	10
deep green	1570	10
deep blue	1566	30
deep rust	1425	10

Madeira Metallic Lurana		
burnt gold	830/425	12

Note: Madeira Metallic Lurana has to be specially ordered.

CANVAS

◆ Cut the canvas, allowing a border of 5 cm (2 in). Bind the edges – *see Canvas, page 138.*
◆ Outline the approximate size and shape of the design with a waterproof indelible marker.
◆ Spray paint the canvas deep red to unify any color showing through.

FOLLOWING THE CHART

◆ The charts show the basic designs and should be repeated as necessary.

STITCHING THE TIEBACK

◆ For instructions, *see Stitching, page 138.*
◆ Use Madeira Metallic Lurana, Madeira Silk, and Madeira Decora as supplied (it is helpful to apply beeswax to the end of the Decora thread).
◆ The overall height should be 12.5 cm (5 in). If a fringe is to be added, this measurement should include the fringe so adjust the design.
◆ The main pattern for the tieback should be stitched first from right to left, the top border and diamond end stitched last. If preferred, rather than using a chenille fringe and Venetian glass beads on the bottom of the tieback, it is possible to repeat the top border pattern.

STITCHING THE PELMET

◆ When starting this pattern, decide which part of the canvas is going to be the center and begin there. From the center work to the left, then to the right, completing one row.

◆ Work one section at a time, leaving the rest of the canvas loosely rolled and held together on either end with large clips.
◆ This pattern should be stitched in sequence with care taken with the stitch lengths as they vary from row to row.
◆ After attaching the chenille fringe, the glass Venetian beads should be individually sewn.

MAKING THE TIEBACK

◆ Select a lining for the back of the tieback – here crimson silk is used. The fringe and glass beads are attached at the end.

MAKING THE PELMET

◆ Unless you are skilled in upholstery, this project should be fabric-lined and mounted by a professional upholsterer – *see page 141.*

Pelmet
Yarn Quantities

Madeira Cotton		Metres
mauve	0811	200
deep rust	0401	100
med. rust	0402	220
dark green	1204	220
deep olive	1312	260
med olive	1407	280
deep mauve	2306	200
apricot	0214	100
blue	1005	240
gold	2211	100

Madeira Decora		
deep rose	1434	80
burgundy	1435	100
deep green	1570	180
blue	1566	260
gold	1425	120

Madeira Metallic Lurana		
burnt gold	830-425	336

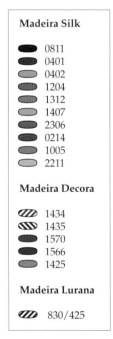

Madeira Silk

- 0811
- 0401
- 0402
- 1204
- 1312
- 1407
- 2306
- 0214
- 1005
- 2211

Madeira Decora

- 1434
- 1435
- 1570
- 1566
- 1425

Madeira Lurana

- 830/425

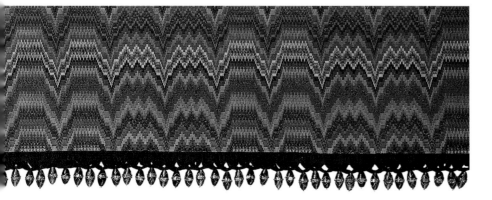

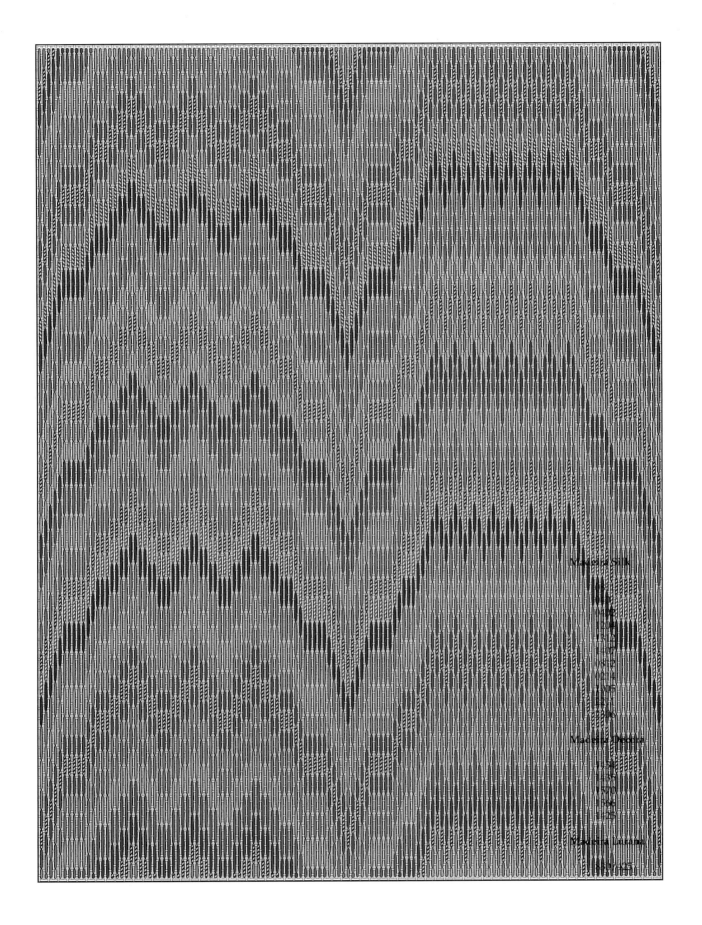

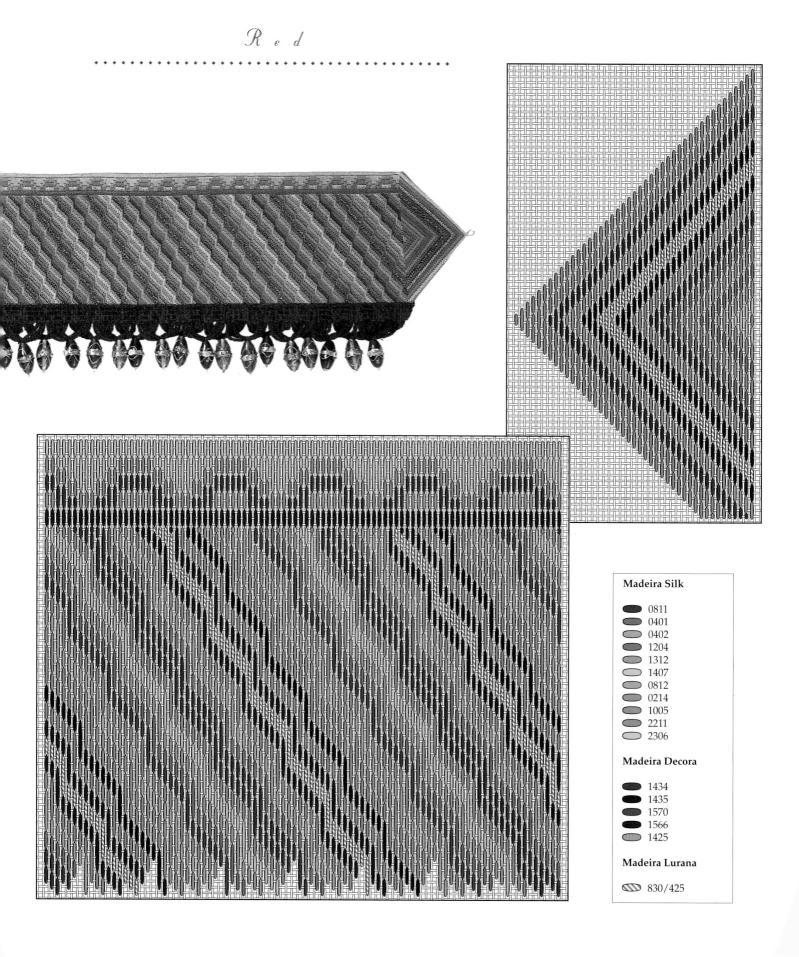

Madeira Silk

- 0811
- 0401
- 0402
- 1204
- 1312
- 1407
- 0812
- 0214
- 1005
- 2211
- 2306

Madeira Decora

- 1434
- 1435
- 1570
- 1566
- 1425

Madeira Lurana

- 830/425

TREES

Trees, a traditional bargello pattern with a three-dimensional effect, is interpreted here in a new way, mixing the softness of lambswool with glistening electric blue glass beads. Its primary warm colors of red and yellow, being tonalities which give back light, appear to come forwards. They create an energy which is active and advancing, corresponding to feelings of assimilation and intensity. The cooler blues and greens relate to the feminine side and seem to recede, evoking feelings of distance.

The graduated color combinations within *Trees* are both energetic and soothing, compatible in creating a comfortable space in which to attain new joy and insight. Its forward energy is dynamic and decisive, transforming ideas into action, while its receding vibrations offer the support of tranquillity and peace. This dynamic dance of opposites creates an attitude of alertness and observation. The clarity of this classic bargello pattern, through its magnetic polarities, feels both restful and stimulating in a composed and decisive way.

Trees enhances all environments because of this harmony in opposites. Its relaxed yet inspiring vibrations are pleasing to the eye, created through its many graduating shades, reminding us that transitions can be graceful and gentle, as well as being co-operative collaborations.

SKILL: average
CANVAS: Madeira 1282/52 antique 13 holes
NEEDLE: tapestry size 18 or 20, bead size 22
SIZE: 46 x 46 cm (18 x 18 in)

OVERLEAF: *There is something about symmetry that evokes harmony, the comfort of everything rational and logical, the feeling of stability and security. Such are the feelings evoked from* Trees, *a pattern stitched for many generations in many countries.*

CANVAS

◆ Cut the canvas, allowing a border of 5 cm (2 in). Bind the edges – *see Canvas, page 138.*

◆ Outline the shape of the design with a water-proof marker, then draw central horizontal and vertical lines to mark the design's center point.

◆ Spray paint the canvas deep brown.

FOLLOWING THE CHART

◆ The chart shows the basic design and should be repeated as necessary.

◆ Thread the two alternating colors belonging to one row, such as red and yellow. Begin at the center of the canvas and work outwards, alternating similarly placed colors, such as the deepest red and deepest yellow shades, and complete these colors in both directions across the canvas. This sequence should be followed throughout the design.

◆ Place the color not being used to the right of the design to avoid the stitching thread.

STITCHING

◆ For instructions, *see Stitching, page 138.*

◆ Use two strands of the Madeira Renaissance Wool doubled.

MAKING THE CUSHION

◆ To complete, *see Finishing, page 139.*

Madeira Renaissance Wool

- ⬭ 1412
- ⬭ 1406
- ⬭ 1413
- ⬭ 1415
- ⬭ 0906
- ⬭ 1622
- ⬭ 1619
- ⬭ 1612
- ⬭ 1613
- ⬭ 1615
- ⬭ 1002
- ⬭ 1003
- ⬭ 1004
- ⬭ 1005
- ⬭ 1006
- ⬭ 1201
- ⬭ 0310
- ⬭ 0402
- ⬭ 1101
- ⬭ 0209
- ⬤ blue glass bead

Yarn Quantities

Madeira Wool		Metres
light gold	1412	13
gold	1406	25
gold	1413	50
gold	1415	50
dark gold	0906	75
light green	1622	13
green	1619	25
green	1612	50
green	1613	50
dark green	1615	75
light blue	1002	13
blue	1003	25
blue	1004	50
blue	1005	50
dark blue	1006	75
light red	1201	13
red	0310	25
red	0402	50
red	1101	50
dark red	0209	75

blue glass bugle beads

GREEN

$\mathcal{M}$ANY LEGENDS SURROUND the feminine color of green which represents all tangibly growing things on the earth. Athena, the Greek goddess of weaving and war, was famed for her green eyes and green robes, often wearing a green emerald on her breastplate. Sacred to her was the green olive. Green was also the fairies' color, providing a protective camouflage for hiding in the woods, while mermaids were renowned for their long sea-green hair.

GREEN

*"I retain from nature a certain sequence and a certain
correctness in placing the tones, I study nature, so as not to do foolish
things, to remain reasonable – however, I don't mind so much
whether my color corresponds exactly, as long as it looks beautiful on
my canvas, as beautiful as it looks in nature."*

VINCENT VAN GOGH, LETTERS TO HIS BROTHER THEO

REEN IS A SERENE and restful color, reminiscent of fields filled with new shoots, high grasslands, luxurious pastures, lush gardens and deep forests. An exhilarating color bringing to the indoors a sense of the outdoors, it symbolizes the freedom of open spaces. Green represents the inexhaustible energy of nature with its equilibrium and harmony, peace and love, expansion and growth, freedom and abundance. Its color radiates the generosity of heart and represents Venus, the goddess of love who brings fruitfulness, contentment and hope. It belongs to the astrological sign Cancer, the feeling side of life.

As a secondary color, green evolves from the mixing of blue and yellow. Its blue extreme is the coolness and tranquillity of turquoise. Its yellow extreme is lime green which evokes warmth, even brilliance. Each combination changes its emotional content according to the additional hues added to the foundation of green, whether emerald green, azure green, sea green, bottle green, apple green, or forest green. Commonly considered a balancing color, green is restful on the eyes, harmonizing with all surroundings.

Green is the heart energy for all life on this planet. Symbolizing harmony of self with the Universe, its endurance and vitality bring peace to our surroundings and

thoughts. Supporting the growth in nature and people, green conveys a sense of strength and stability, unity and renewal which rejoices in new life. As a gentle healing vibration, green imparts hope and understanding, integrity and compassion and reflects the eternal cycle of life and death.

The open spaces of green permit every aspect of a situation to be seen, encouraging resolution and direction in life. Its opposite challenge is a need for space, difficulties in decision-making, jealousy when green with envy which desires another's space. Emotionally, green helps to calm anxiety, and stimulates both heart and lungs, protects the immune system, energizes the thymus gland, promotes positive feelings of compassion and sensitivity. Its essential oils are pine, bergamot and melissa. Its stones are emerald, tourmaline, malachite, green agate, green jade and beryl.

As a discreet color, green enhances rooms where peace and calmness are desired, bringing security, protection and harmony. Such environments provide us with the space to find our own way, free us of old ideas and help with decision-making on all levels. As a color which supports heart rather than head, green brings clarity of communication to feelings by helping us to remember. It encourages new beginnings and the release of the old, enhancing the desire to see everything in balance. As an intermediate, transitional color it both hides and reveals, and offers the richness and inspiration of life everlasting.

AUTUMN

Green, a variable and versatile palette of over a hundred different shades, contains incredible nuances that reflect richness and abundance, balance and harmony within nature. A color peaceful and restful to the eye, green provides an excellent contemplative background.

The design *Autumn* speaks to greens of the forest, their tones varying from deep fir greens to muted celadon greens, from the silver green of rosemary and sage to the sap green of trees. Here its complementary tones of red, being warm and advancing, appear closer than the greens that surround them. The deep purple, whose base is red and blue, feels passive and retreating.

This color combination creates a nostalgic mood reminiscent of wandering through the forest in the late afternoon when the sun is leaving. It reflects a time to look within, to discover one's inner strength. Its emotional content, amidst the nourishment of nature, permits one to review life through quiet contemplation. Its introspective vibration allows the space in which to find oneself. The energy of *Autumn* is of quiet transformation, of re-evaluating and beginning anew, the time when the change of season offers a change of direction, when both the mind and body are renewed.

Such a chair enhances a quiet corner, a place of repose where *Autumn* encourages contemplation in the comfort of one's surroundings. Its sense is not of isolation but rather preparation before deciding upon possible choices. Nothing dramatic or dynamic happens here, as the peace and tranquillity of accepting leisure space is offered in which to nourish new decisions.

SKILL: average
CANVAS: Madeira 1282/70 antique 18 holes
NEEDLE: tapestry size 18 or 20
SIZE: 60 x 60 cm (24 x 24 in)

RIGHT: *How can one not respect the silence of the season when leaves fall and greens become dense and sombre, when a sense of winter's coming can be felt in the cool night air. Such feelings are evoked by Autumn's colors whose center pattern is as a path through the woods, whose right and left sides are the same, aware of coming changes, whose wool threads offer the comfort of warmth for winter.*

Yarn Quantities

Madeira Wool		Metres
deep green	1615	75
med green	1613	50
aubergine	0203	75
deep olive	1510	50
med olive	1516	50
light green	1612	125
light olive	1515	125

Madeira Cotton		
deep rust	2501	35
crimson	0514	30
crimson	2606	35

Madeira Metallic Glamour		
greens	9804/2500	171

CANVAS

◆ Cut the canvas to the desired rectangular size, allowing a border of at least 7.5 cm (3 in) all around for handling and finishing.

◆ Tape or stitch all four sides to prevent fraying – *see Canvas, page 138* for details.

◆ Outline the approximate size and shape of the design with a tested, waterproof indelible ink marker, then draw central horizontal and vertical lines. The design's center point is where the lines cross.

◆ Using a green fast-drying spray enamel paint, spray paint across the canvas surface to unify any color showing through.

FOLLOWING THE CHART

◆ An original variation of an old Florentine pattern, this design is based on flames and zigzags, the right and left sides mirroring each other. Its motif is uncomplicated as the first row establishes the pattern and all subsequent rows follow in sequential order.

◆ The chart shows the basic design for this chair cushion and should be repeated as many times as necessary to cover the canvas.

◆ This pattern can be adjusted to any size or shape desired. As a single motif design, work each row from the right to left, beginning at the bottom right-hand corner until each horizontal row is completed. Finish the lower half of the stitching first, then reverse the canvas to complete the upper half.

STITCHING

◆ For detailed stitching instructions, *see Stitching, page 138.*

◆ Use Madeira 6 Stranded Cotton as supplied. Use two strands of Madeira Renaissance Wool doubled. Use Madeira Metallic doubled.

MAKING THE CHAIR SEAT COVER

◆ When following the pattern for a corner seat cover, the finished design needs to be cut into a triangular shape, leaving at least 7.5 cm (3 in) of blank canvas all around for upholstery. Unless you are experienced in finishing a chair seat cover, it is recommended that the bargello chair be completed by a professional upholsterer.

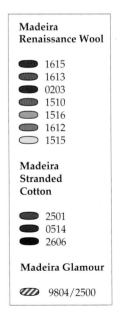

Madeira Renaissance Wool

- 1615
- 1613
- 0203
- 1510
- 1516
- 1612
- 1515

Madeira Stranded Cotton

- 2501
- 0514
- 2606

Madeira Glamour

- 9804/2500

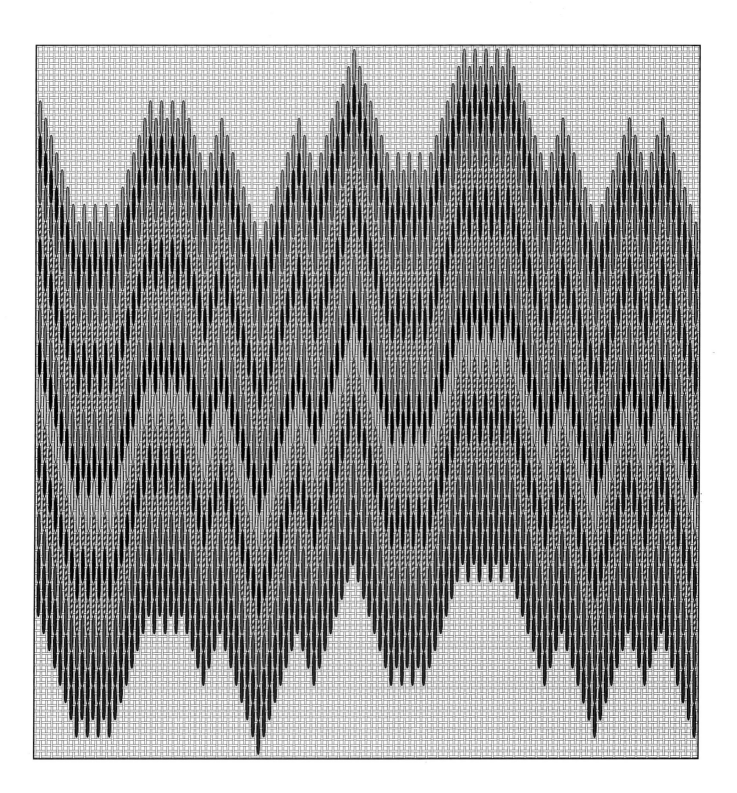

EMERALD MAZE

Emerald Maze, a distinctive bargello pattern of basketweave design, is most effective when variations of the same color are shaded from light to dark. Such color combinations change dramatically according to each adjacent color. In *Emerald Maze*, a green base color belongs to all the threads.

In one section of four interlocking rows, yellow has been added to the green base, thus the chosen colors vary from lime green to ochre. These green-yellow combinations evoke feelings of warmth, intimacy and wisdom. They are heart-centered and bring calmness to difficult situations, easing claustrophobic conditions as one seeks the right space and right place. In its opposite section of four interlocking rows are emerald green shades whose green-blue combinations are cool, expansive and peaceful. These colors represent the state of relaxation in which one feels the growth of space, the tranquillity of meadows and green grass, the revitalizing and opening of the heart.

The many-layered emotions aroused by such opposing color combinations are represented by the multi-dimensional effect of the pattern itself. *Emerald Maze* is both an intimate and distant cushion whose vibrancy, resulting from warm colors opposing cool colors, draws attention to itself wherever it is placed. Within an environment it brings a sense that similarities and opposition exist simultaneously, reminding one that choice is necessary and available at every given moment. The luxury of such knowledge sparkles with green glass beads, suggesting life is best as a joy not a struggle.

SKILL: average
CANVAS: Madeira 1282/52 antique 13 holes
NEEDLE: tapestry size 18 or 20, bead size 22
SIZE: 35 x 43 cm (14 x 17 in)

RIGHT: *This classic lattice pattern has always symbolized the intertwining of life, the weaving together of people and the events they share. The choice of multiple shades of the same color green evokes feelings of sharing while being separate, of being independent yet having a group identity. Here such complexity is accentuated by using two shades of green glass beads to form a pattern within a pattern.*

Yarn Quantities

Madeira Silk		Metres
light green	1706	20
green	1204	20
green	1214	20
light green	1212	20
dark green	1312	20
green	1407	20
green	1408	20
light green	1409	20

round glass beads in emerald
and dark emerald green

CANVAS

◆ Cut the canvas, allowing a border of 5 cm (2 in). Bind the edges – *see Canvas, page 138*.
◆ Outline the design with a waterproof indelible marker, then draw central horizontal and vertical lines.
◆ Spray paint the canvas green to unify any color showing through.

FOLLOWING THE CHART

◆ The pattern is created with parallel stitches following in diagonal rows, each row containing 12 stitches. The interlocking rows in one direction are worked in four shades of yellow-green. The interlocking rows crossing them are four shades of emerald green. The squares are filled with two shades of green beads to enhance the multi-dimensional effect.

◆ The chart shows the basic design and should be repeated as necessary.
◆ When starting, thread all needles with the complete color sequence, i.e. eight green shades graded from light to dark. Begin at the center and work outwards, stitching all twelve stitches of each color to establish the base of the four row sequence.
◆ The colors not being used should be placed to the right of the design so as not to interfere with the stitching thread.

STITCHING

◆ For instructions, *see Stitching, page 138*. When stitching is complete, sew the glass beads on individually – *see Beading, page 139*.
◆ Use Madeira Silk doubled.

MAKING THE CUSHION

◆ To complete, *see Finishing, page 139*.

Madeira Silk

- 1706
- 1204
- 1214
- 1212
- 1312
- 1407
- 1408
- 1409

- ○ light green glass bead
- ● dark green glass bead

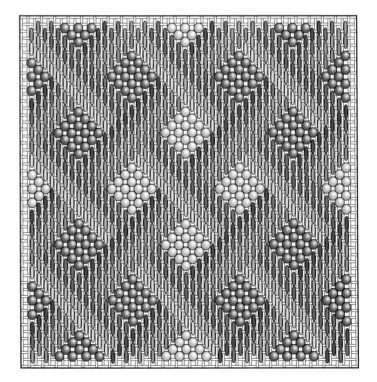

SPRINGTIME

Color begins with nature, and nature is what all our personal color memories and reactions have in common. *Springtime* is purposely a nostalgic design, drawing you towards colors which recall places once known, gardens and flowers remembered. Its colors remind us of other times, perhaps colors of

childhood places or of gardens and forests which left impressions that seem to stay forever. The use of such sentimental colors inspires feelings and moods which can evoke powerful insights.

As the quality of color depends on the quality of light illuminating it, a bargello lampshade requires particular attention. Objects that are brightened at night need deeper, stronger colors to offset the yellowing effect of light bulbs. Such density of color has the power to transform the smallest space into a vibrant and enriching ambience.

Here the background consists of subtle shadings of olive green, reminiscent of mature olives growing on trees, evoking feelings of harmony with nature in a simple, modest way. Essentially a dark color, olive green is a muted tone consisting of warm yellow and green. Its dense earthy hues are a superb background for the brighter, luxurious colors of the surrounding flowers.

The *Springtime* lampshade is a subtle statement about incorporating past memories into present time, integrating the warmth held in one's heart with everyday activities. Its design addresses the acceptance of seasons and change, of cherishing flowers in full bloom while honoring the ever-present shadow of deep green.

SKILL: advanced
CANVAS: Madeira 1282/70 antique 18 holes
NEEDLE: tapestry size 20
SIZE: for a 25 cm (10 in) diameter lampshade –
canvas size 37 x 60 cm (14½ x 24 in)

Yarn Quantities

Madeira Decora		Metres
dark green	1570	35

Madeira Silk		
dark green	1705	30
dark green	1314	25
dark green	1405	30
light green	1212	15
med green	1214	15
red	0506	5
red	0206	5
red	0210	5
red	0511	5
lilac	0711	5
lilac	0713	5
lilac	0902	5
lilac	0803	5
terracotta	0402	5
terracotta	0811	5
terracotta	0214	5
terracotta	0403	5
gold	0303	5
gold	0812	5
gold	2307	5
gold	0113	5

CANVAS

◆ Cut a canvas piece 37 x 60 cm (14½ x 24 in). This allows for a border of 5 cm (2 in) all around for finishing into a 25 cm (10 in) lampshade.

◆ Tape or stitch a binding on all sides to prevent fraying.

◆ Outline a rectangle 27 x 50 cm (10½ x 20 in) with a tested, waterproof indelible ink marker. Make a mark 16.5 cm (6½ in) from the top right-hand corner on the horizontal line, and then repeat from the top left-hand corner. In the remaining space, at its center point, draw a vertical line which divides the canvas into two parts. On this vertical line from the top downwards mark 10 cm (4 in) which represents the top circumference of the lampshade. Draw a semi-circle between these three points.

◆ Draw a second semi-circle from the upper right to the upper left-hand corner, of the canvas to the base of this center vertical line. This establishes the approximate shape of the lampshade pattern. The canvas now has two distinct sections: A on the left and B on the right. Divide each in half to form two further sections: C and D on the left and E and F on the right. This creates four sections C, D, E and F.

◆ At the intersections of C-E and E-F sew a white thread (later removed) to mark these divisions. In rotating the canvas, the sections between D-E and C-F are where the canvas threads are horizontal.

◆ Using a medium green fast-drying spray enamel paint, spray across the canvas surface to unify any color showing through.

◆ When not stitching always roll the canvas, design outwards, to avoid distortion from folding.

FOLLOWING THE CHART

◆ This pattern is a variation of four-way bargello but here only one side, rather than the traditional four sides, requires the mitred design – *see Stitching, page 138.*

◆ The design given here is one-quarter of the pattern (C) for this 25 cm (10 in) lampshade and should be stitched one complete section at a time.

LEFT: *Using a variation of the four-way bargello pattern permitted this semi-circular shape to be created, the canvas remaining horizontal for stitching its design. Here a geometric bargello pattern harmonizes with needlepoint long and short stitches to define each flower, permitting curved shapes to be created. This combination of needlepoint and bargello has been used for centuries, always adding versatility to its style.*

STITCHING

◆ The instruction chart represents section C, the upper part of section A.

◆ Start at its lower right-hand corner and stitch the pattern from right to left. Then reverse the canvas and stitch the section D, changing the flower colors accordingly, and continue stitching until E is completed.

◆ Turn the canvas completely around to stitch section F, changing the flower colors. Where sections C-D and E-F meet, the divisions are indicated by a sewn white threads (later removed). Here the bargello stitching is mitred – *see Stitching page 138.*

◆ For detailed stitching instructions, *see Stitching page 138*

◆ Use Madeira Silk and Madeira Decora as supplied (it is helpful to apply beeswax to the end of the Madeira Decora thread).

MAKING THE LAMPSHADE

◆ Unless you are skilled at such finishing, this lampshade should be fabric-lined and framed by a professional lampshade maker familiar with handling canvas or textiles – *see Suppliers' Addresses, page 141.*

Madeira Silk

background:
 1570 (Decora)
1705
1314
1405

green leaves:
1212
1214

red flower:
0506
0206
0210
0511

lilac flower:
0711
0713
0902
0803

terracotta flower:
0402
0811
0214
0403

gold flower:
0303
0812
2307
0113

➤ seams

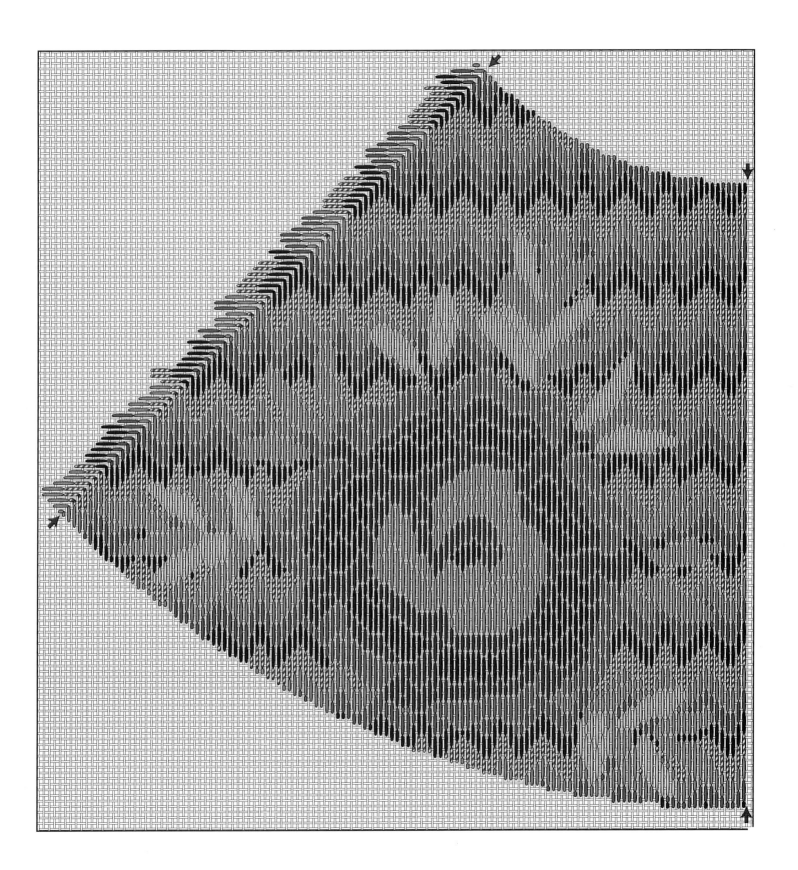

BYZANTINE

Byzantine is created from a curved row that mirrors itself, which then forms a series of circular medallions. The open spaces between these motifs become a secondary pattern of small, curved diamond shapes. Here the mood of the composition contrasts intense greens, from soft green to turquoise green to deep green, against warm red and cool blue medallions.

Just as green symbolizes space, freedom and the search for truth, so its complementary color red seeks activity and passion. Its opposite colors are blue, which brings serenity and peacefulness, and gold, which signifies wisdom and love. The interaction of these supportive colors creates an atmosphere of inviting warmth, tranquillity and resolution. Its combination broadens one's horizons. Green comforts the healing heart, representing new beginnings after overcoming deep fears. Its overall vibration is forgiveness of self and others, helping to bring forth an optimistic view of life.

Yarn Quantities

Madeira Silk		Metres
blue	1711	10
deep blue	1712	30
red	0511	25
mauve	0811	10
dark green	1705	85
green	1204	95
olive green	1312	85
olive	1407	80
brown	2113	35
light green	1510	65
Madeira Metallic		
gold	9803/3004	140

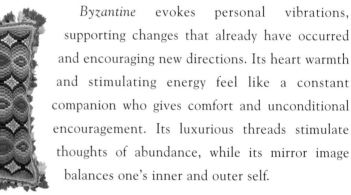

Byzantine evokes personal vibrations, supporting changes that already have occurred and encouraging new directions. Its heart warmth and stimulating energy feel like a constant companion who gives comfort and unconditional encouragement. Its luxurious threads stimulate thoughts of abundance, while its mirror image balances one's inner and outer self.

OVERLEAF: *When colors are skilfully chosen, it is difficult to believe that such a visually complex bargello design derives from a simple source. This classic pattern becomes elegant from combining threads of silk and gold. For a luxurious effect, care must be taken to ensure that the silk and gold threads are smooth and not twisted.*

SKILL: beginner/average
CANVAS: Madeira 1282/56 antique 15 hole
NEEDLE: tapestry size 18 or 20
SIZE: 30 x 63 cm (11¾ x 25 in)

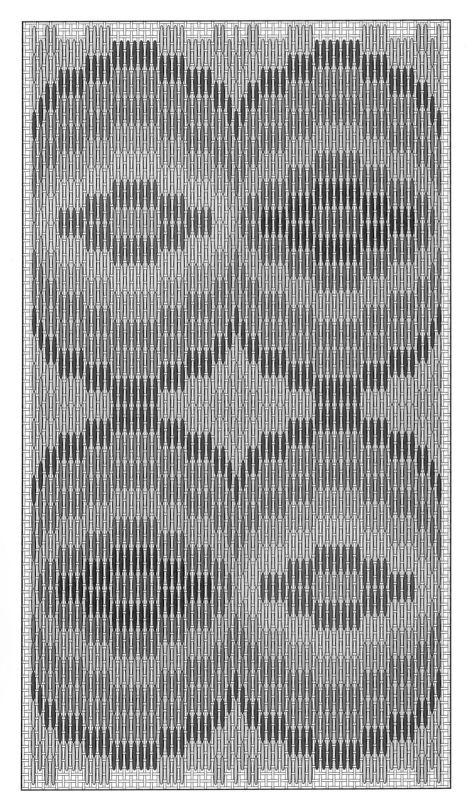

CANVAS

◆ Cut the canvas, allowing a border of 5 cm (2 in). Bind the edges – *see Canvas, page 138.*

◆ Outline the size and shape of the design with a waterproof indelible marker, then draw central horizontal and vertical lines. The design's center point is where these lines cross.

◆ Spray paint the canvas green to unify any color showing through.

FOLLOWING THE CHART

◆ This original design is a variation of traditional Florentine canvaswork. The first row establishes the pattern with subsequent rows following. Upon reaching the center of each medallion, the design reverses as a mirror image.

◆ The stitch chart shows the basic design for this cushion and should be repeated as necessary. This pattern can be adjusted to suit any size or shape.

◆ Always begin at the center of the canvas, working in both directions until an entire horizontal row of pattern has been established. Complete the lower half first, then reverse the canvas to complete the upper half.

STITCHING

◆ For instructions, *see Stitching, page 138.*

◆ Use Madeira Silk and Madeira Metallic doubled.

MAKING THE CUSHION

◆ For instructions *see Finishing, page 139.*

Madeira Silk

- 1711
- 1712
- 0511
- 0811
- 1705
- 1204
- 1312
- 1407
- 2113
- 1510

Madeira Metallic

- 9803/3004

B L U E

$\mathcal{B}$LUE HAS TRADITIONALLY represented truth and all things exalted. In Egypt, mummies were painted blue, to be united with the soul of truth. Its stone of lapis lazuli symbolized the truth, while the sapphire blue stone represented intuition and telepathic powers. The tablets Moses received on Mount Sinai were believed to be of blue sapphire, indicative of their divine origin. For many ancient religions, blue epitomized devotion and adoration, sincerity and spirituality. Sky blue was the color of the Great Mother, the Queen of Heaven, and of all sky gods and sky powers.

BLUE

"The deep blue sky was flecked with clouds of a blue deeper than the
fundamental blue of intense cobalt, and others of a clearer blue,
like the blue whiteness of the Milky Way. In the blue depth the stars
were sparkling, greenish, yellow, white, rose, brighter, flashing
more like jewels, than they do at home – even in Paris; opals you might
call them, emeralds, lapis, rubies, sapphires."

VINCENT VAN GOGH, LETTERS TO HIS BROTHER THEO

BLUE IS A MYSTERIOUS spiritual color which penetrates the depths of the sea and the far reaches of the sky. It symbolizes the coolness of waters below and heavens above and brings about a mood which is calming, relaxing and soothing without the influence of sensuality or intellect. As a color of endless space and expansion, blue encompasses all that is peaceful and ethereal, gentle and tender. It is a meditative energy which relaxes the mind and stimulates thoughts toward spiritual and psychological matters. Its seeming contradiction between repose and expansion, hiding and revealing, in actuality means taking quiet space to expand one's deepest feelings and highest concepts. The energy of blue addresses truth and devotion, tranquillity and sincerity, loyalty and reliability.

The person who is true blue and blue-blooded brings consistency, a sense of duty and honor, courtesy and calm, harmony and happiness. Faith and contemplation, serenity and prudence are

its attributes, associated with a sense of formality and tradition. As the quality of blue is soothing and soft, so it encourages meditation and all forms of prayer, assisting both spiritual and physical communication. It calms the mind, soothes the nerves, slows down the pulse rate and lowers blood pressure, brings about a relaxing almost sedative effect to the thymus and thyroid glands. Associated with the throat, it is the creative center of man, concerned with the speech of communication and self-expression.

The colors of blue are infinite and expansive, with many more tonalities than words can name. In general, pale blue symbolizes simplicity, innocence and candor, electric blue personal magnetism, deep blue spirituality, indigo blue intuition and spiritual perception. Its enormous color range encompasses sky blue, slate blue, Wedgwood blue, navy blue, Prussian blue, ultramarine and cobalt blue, azure and denim blue to identify but a few. Its stones are lapis lazuli, known for its supernatural beauty and perfection, sapphire, the stone of saints, healers and yogis, as well as turquoise and aquamarine. Its flowers include bluebells, periwinkles, gentians, hyacinths, cornflowers, morning glory and lavender.

Blue is an uplifting, ascending color whose intensity of coolness or warmth varies with the amount of red or green within each shade. The vibrancy and strength within each color creates a different mood dependent upon surrounding colors or other tones mixed within. Turquoise blue, which has much green in it, becomes a cool shade of blue. Whereas cobalt blue and ultramarine, mauves and lavenders, having a certain amount of red within them, become warm blues. Yet in all instances blue stands for divinity, protection, intuition and serenity.

FLORENTINE FLOWER BOX

The *Florentine Flower Box* is a festival of vibrant and spirited colors, a celebration of energies and harmonious feelings. Its widely differing colors enhance one another, creating an exhilarating and inspiring effect, accessing imagination and creativity, and bringing happiness into the home. Its deep, warm blue background supports other strong colors, providing a lustrous, striking contrast.

With the complementary color of deep orange, blue allows the rich tonalities of coral, rust, red, violet and purple, as well as stimulating greens, to sparkle like jewels. Their bright, exuberant tones lend luminosity to the composition. These highly versatile and adaptable colors portray an exceptional elegance and refinement coupled with understated clarity and vividness.

The emotional context of the *Florentine Flower Box* is one of enhancing creativity, using intuitive talents to achieve success through nurturing passionate feelings. The blue and red combination transforms ideas into action, sees things clearly, and understands the quality of life. Blue combined with violet and purple brings warmth while achieving results, enhancing dynamic and unconventional relationships. Green foliage nourishes heart communication, as expressed in the emerald glass beads.

Such a design enjoys prominent placement within harmonious and stimulating surroundings. It brings vitality and awareness into an atmosphere, the delight of space and dynamic interaction, as well as being an object of beauty in itself.

SKILL: advanced
CANVAS: Madeira 1282/52 antique 13 holes
NEEDLE: tapestry size 18 or 20, bead size 22
SIZE: 30 x 30 x 14 cm (12 x 12 x 5½ in)

RIGHT: *One of the most rewarding extensions of contemporary stitching is created when the bargello technique becomes a mitred design, commonly referred to as four-way bargello.*

Yarn Quantities

Madeira Decora		Metres
light green	1501	15
med green	1450	5
dark green	1449	20
deep rose	1434	20
red	1439	25
burgundy	1435	80
lilac	1433	20
purple	1480	130
med blue	1534	200
dark blue	1575	140

CANVAS

◆ Cut the canvas in a 35.5 cm (14 in) square. This allows 5 cm (2 in) border. Bind the edges.

◆ Within the canvas outline a 30 cm (12 in) square with a waterproof marker. From each corner draw a diagonal line, the center point being where these lines cross. With a white thread (later removed), stitch over these lines.

◆ Spray paint the canvas medium blue to unify any color showing through.

FOLLOWING THE CHART

◆ Each chart shows the basic design for this four-way bargello, to be repeated as necessary.

STITCHING

◆ Complete one triangular section at a time (one quarter of the design), stitching into the holes of the white threads. Rotate each section 90 degrees so the base line forms the horizontal rows to be stitched. The white thread represents a mitred corner –*see Stitching, page 138*.

◆ Use Madeira Decora doubled.

◆ When the sections are finished, fill in small stitches where needed, then stitch the border.

◆ On a separate canvas stitch the base pattern, primarily one horizontal row that is followed accordingly, with the border being stitched last.

◆ For instructions, *see Stitching, page 138*. To apply the beads, *see Beading, page 139*.

MAKING THE WOOD BOX

◆ It is advisable to have this box velvet-lined and framed by an upholsterer, *see page 141*.

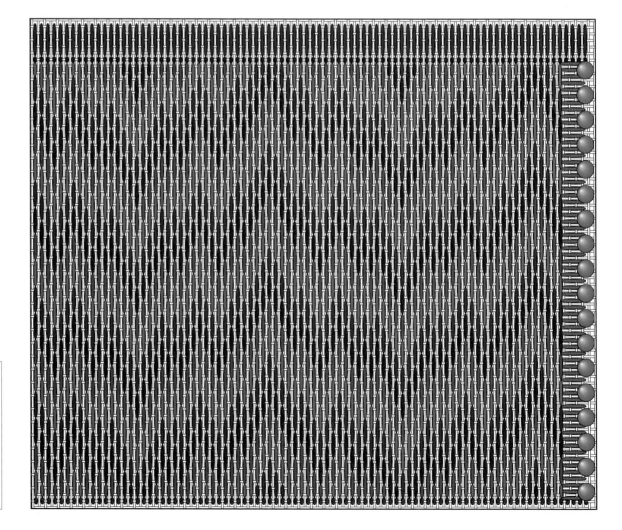

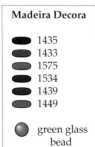

Madeira Decora

- 1435
- 1433
- 1575
- 1534
- 1439
- 1449
- green glass bead

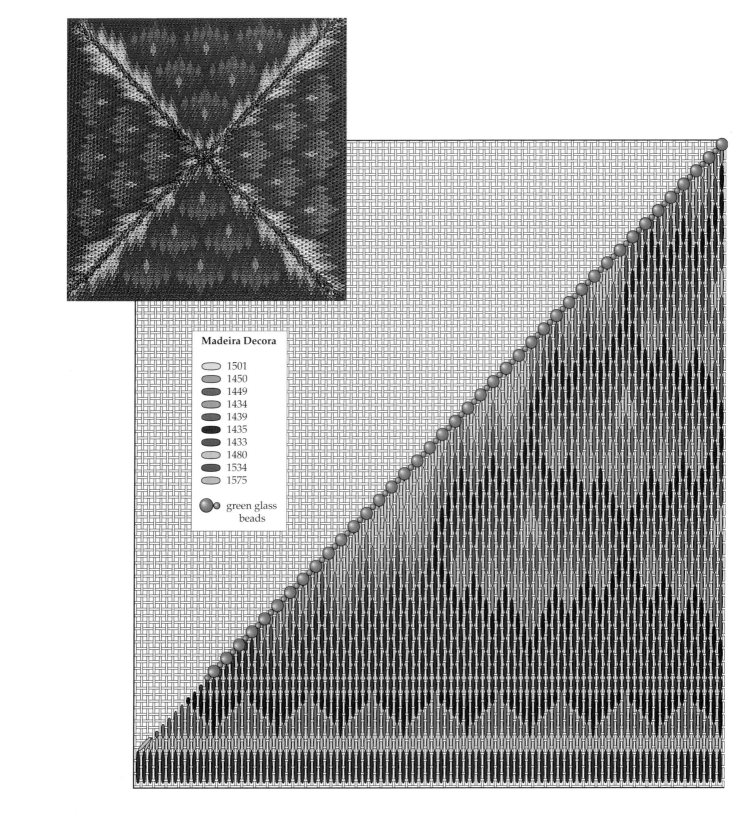

Madeira Decora

- 1501
- 1450
- 1449
- 1434
- 1439
- 1435
- 1433
- 1480
- 1534
- 1575

green glass beads

GARLAND

The dominant mood of *Garland* is relaxing, soothing and contemplative for creativity. Its blue colors are attuned to psychic and physical communication, while its red vitality helps to express these subtle energies. This interplay of blue and red brings about peace and renewal, combining the spiritual energy of blue with the active emotions of red.

This color combination reflects an individual committed to peace within and without, dedicated to harmony and developing personal artistic talents, especially for success later in life. It reveals deep instincts and psychic awareness, as blue's strength of silence requires introspection where intuitive knowledge can activate the imagination.

Reflecting the light, warm blues of hyacinths and cornflowers, these tones are gentle and soothing, welcoming and easy to live with. Coupled with greens, this graceful pattern enhances an ambience for both private and public space. Its dynamic red colors excite the passive, intuitive blue with its tendency towards contentment and timelessness to achieve results.

Garland is a cushion which balances activity with peacefulness. It inspires projects to be completed, and enjoys the freshness of nature with the pleasure of expansion. Enriching thoughts and creativity, it enhances a space of mental activity, as well as communication between individuals. Its intrinsic harmony heightens endeavors of collaboration, especially in the innovative stage of projects.

SKILL: beginner
CANVAS: Madeira 1282/52 antique, 13 holes
NEEDLES: tapestry size 18 or 20
SIZE: 71 x 28 cm (28 x 11 in)

RIGHT: *The joy of bargello stitching is a return to the instinctive handling of vivid and subtle colors within rich geometric patterns, skills inherited from generations long past. As this method of stitching is intuitive and meditative, it encourages relaxation and contemplation.*

Yarn Quantities

Madeira Silk		Metres
red	0511	100
rust	0811	65
grey blue	1714	45
med blue grey	1712	45
light blue grey	1711	45
dark green	1204	40
med green	1311	20
deep green	1405	45
med olive	1312	45
light olive	1407	45
deep blue	1005	40
dark blue	1003	20

CANVAS

◆ Cut the canvas to the desired size, allowing a border of 5 cm (2 in) all around for finishing.

◆ Tape or stitch all four sides to prevent fraying – *see Canvas, page 138* for details.

◆ Outline the approximate size and shape of the design with a tested, waterproof indelible ink marker, then draw central horizontal and vertical lines to make four equal sections. The design's center point is where these lines cross.

◆ Using a blue fast-drying spray enamel paint, spray across the canvas surface to unify any color showing through.

FOLLOWING THE CHART

◆ This original design is a variation of traditional Florentine canvas work that combines domes and spires, also known as scallops and flames. Its motif is uncomplicated as the first row establishes the pattern, with all subsequent rows merely following.

◆ The stitch chart shows the basic design for this cushion and should be repeated as many times as necessary to complete the example stitched. This pattern can be adjusted to any size or shape desired.

◆ As a single motif design, work each row from the right to left, beginning at the bottom right-hand corner until each horizontal row is completed.

◆ Finish the lower half of the stitching first, then reverse the canvas to complete the upper half of the design.

STITCHING

◆ For detailed stitching instructions, *see Stitching, page 138.*

◆ Use Madeira Silk doubled.

MAKING THE CUSHION

◆ For instructions on completing this bargello cushion, *see Finishing, page 139.*

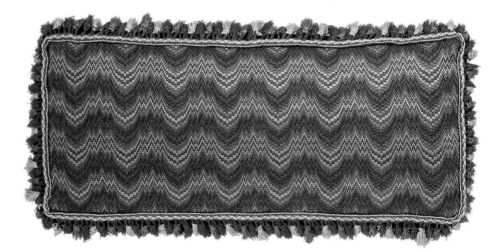

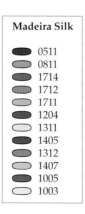

Madeira Silk	
⬤	0511
⬤	0811
⬤	1714
⬤	1712
⬤	1711
⬤	1204
⬤	1311
⬤	1405
⬤	1312
⬤	1407
⬤	1005
⬤	1003

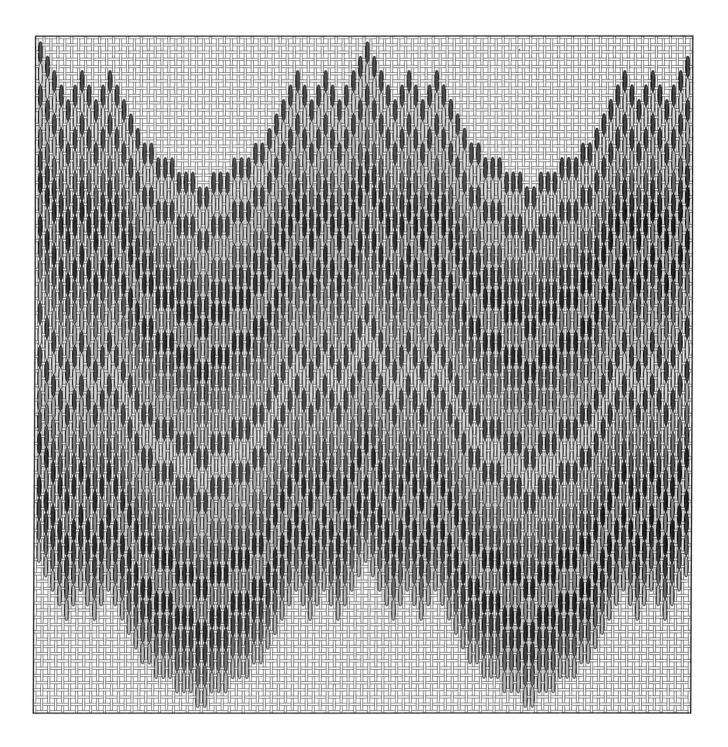

GAMBLER'S DELIGHT

Gambler's Delight is for those enthused about taking chances, excited by the risk of the edge. Its blue depends upon intuition to access knowledge, highlighting the emotions of the reckless and daring. Here turquoise blue holds the personal magnetism needed to draw towards oneself the energy desired

in any given situation. The red hearts and diamonds bring grounding energy, passion and abundance, while its red traffic light warns of direct danger. Such dynamic emotion understands stress and chaos, frustration and aggression. The black clubs and spades accept darkness and despair yet are enticed by the mystery of things hidden.

Turquoise thrives in expansive undefined space. Here psychic abilities and deep memory live in the moment. Exuding coolness, turquoise makes the impossible seem possible, contemplates before acting, exercises free will to achieve outrageous but carefully thought out decisions. Turquoise with gold represents power, wisdom and the deep fear of deception and delusion that incites nervousness and confusion. Yet, its sense of illumination absorbs harmful vibrations and expands feelings of the marvellous and desirable, trusting intuition and easily adjusting to change.

The excitement of *Gambler's Delight* comes from its silky elegance coupled with a dignified yet eye-catching design. Its appearance immediately evokes passion and love for the crisis of challenge. It offers no solutions, only the cards of chance and the acceptance of whichever deck is dealt.

SKILL: advanced
CANVAS: Madeira 1282/70 antique 18 holes
NEEDLE: tapestry size 20
SIZE: average

OVERLEAF: *Within geometric designs the frivolity of fantasy can be created. Gamblers' Delight, stitched with luxurious silk and gold threads, evokes feelings of extravagance and excess. It attracts attention with a lightness of humor yet with the sophistication of style.*

Yarn Quantities

Madeira Silk		Metres
turquoise	1102	35
med blue	1107	40
grey blue	1005	40
med blue	1103	45
black	black	60
red	0511	65

Madeira Metallic		
gold	5015/9805	60

CANVAS

◆ If you wish, you can buy a dressmaking pattern for the vest (waistcoat) and use this for cutting out the canvas fronts. The pattern should not have any darts.

◆ Cut the canvas to the desired size, allowing a border of 5 cm (2 in) all around for finishing.

◆ Tape or stitch all four sides to prevent fraying – *see Canvas, page 138* for details.

◆ Outline the approximate size and shape of the design with a tested, waterproof indelible ink marker.

◆ Using a blue fast-drying spray enamel paint, spray across the canvas surface to unify any color showing through.

FOLLOWING THE CHART

◆ The motif given here is the basic design for this vest (waistcoat) and should be repeated as many times as necessary to complete your desired size.

STITCHING

◆ This design is not difficult but requires careful attention in counting the canvas threads – a necessity in mastering the Hungarian point stitch.

◆ The gold metallic thread should be used doubled and is stitched first as its outline establishes the pattern throughout. This should be followed by each separate section stitched according to the instruction chart. The color pattern is as follows:

0511 red heart with 1005 blue background
0511 red diamond with 1103 blue background
black club with 1102 blue background
black spade with 1107 blue background

◆ The example shown here has been stitched for a medium/average size and can be altered by extending or reducing the design as required.

◆ For detailed stitching instructions, *see Stitching, page 138.*

◆ Use Madeira Silk as supplied. Use Madeira Metallic doubled.

MAKING UP THE VEST

◆ To complete the vest (waistcoat), black satin has been used for the lining fabric and black velvet for the outside, trimmed with a fine black metallic braid. Unless you are an experienced dressmaker, it is highly recommended that the vest is completed by a professional seamstress – *see Suppliers' Addresses, page 141.*

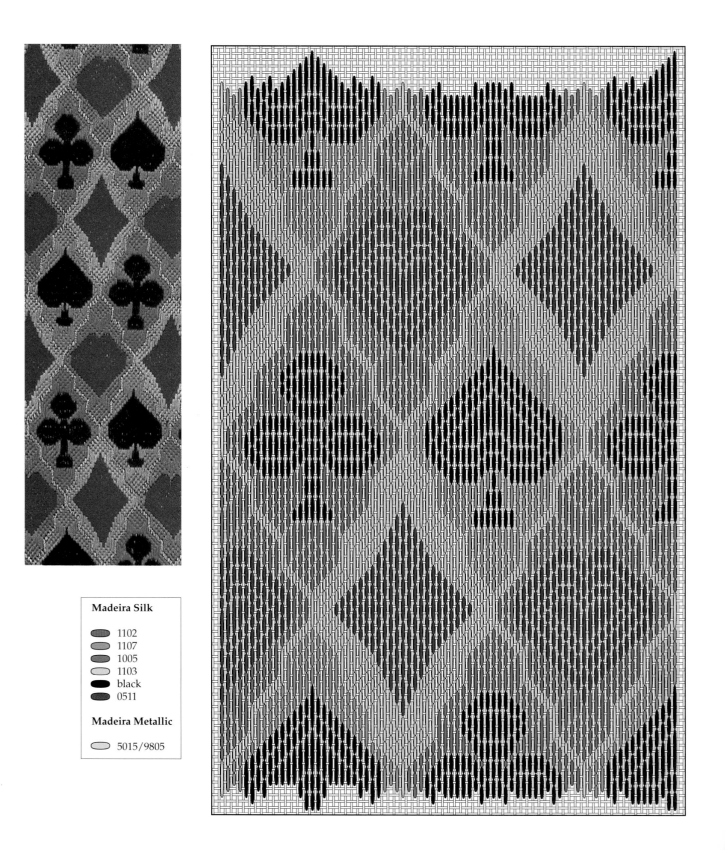

Madeira Silk

- 1102
- 1107
- 1005
- 1103
- black
- 0511

Madeira Metallic

- 5015/9805

TWISTS

Through braiding colors and intermingling tonalities, *Twists* uses a traditional bargello technique of exploring graduating colors. Here the variations of blue have surreal qualities which juxtapose excitement and tranquillity, obscuring yet revealing emotions about something that looks substantial but is not. The intangibility of blue feels unreal and not of this world, invoking ideas of eternity and infinite potential.

Blue represents the expansion of air and water, generating a supreme sense of well being. A color of meditation and deciphering dreams, blue remains elusive and evasive. Its spiritual concern is for love and truth, loyalty and reliability. Its receptive and passive qualities retain the illusion that exceptional things happen 'once in a blue moon'. Here the deeper blues in *Twists* are distant, luminous blues recalling the day and night sky with its infinite ethereal qualities, its contemplation and tranquillity. The vibrant turquoise blues recall waterfalls and rivers with their emotional coolness and distance. The effect of both gives a feeling of greater space than actually exists.

This design complements an environment which encourages one's imagination to soar, to bring thoughts from the space of dreams, to capture feelings of loftiness and distance. Its mood is peaceful, its spirit mysterious. It enhances quiet spaces for contemplation and internal thoughts, inspiring one to reach beyond the limits of daily life.

SKILL: average
CANVAS: Madeira 1282/70 antique 18 holes
NEEDLE: tapestry size 20
SIZE: 56 x 46 cm (22 x 28 in)

OVERLEAF: *Using variations within graduated blue tones,* Twists *creates a complementary background for other colors and objects. The effect of undulating columns creates an animated surface that is stimulating through its movement while evoking the tranquillity of blue.*

109

Yarn Quantities

Madeira Decora		Metres
aqua dark	1585	57
aqua	1490	57
aqua	1446	57
aqua	1445	57
light aqua	1501	57
dark blue	1534	64
blue	1575	64
blue	1495	64
blue	1533	64
light blue	1475	64

CANVAS

◆ Cut the canvas, allowing a border of 5 cm (2 in). Bind the edges – *see Canvas, page 138.*
◆ Outline the design's shape with a waterproof indelible marker, then draw central horizontal and vertical lines to mark the design's center.
◆ Spray paint the canvas medium blue to unify any color showing through – *see page 138.*

FOLLOWING THE CHART

◆ The chart shows the basic design and should be repeated as necessary.
◆ Thread eight needles with the complete color sequence – four variations of blue and four of blue-green, graduated from light to dark.
◆ Begin at the bottom center and work upwards, stitching all four colors of each section until its sequence is established.
◆ Place the colors not being used out of the way to the right of the design.

STITCHING

◆ For instructions, *see Stitching page 138.*
◆ Use Madeira Decora as supplied.

MAKING THE FRAME

◆ Ask a professional framer to complete the frame – *see Suppliers' Addresses, page 141.*

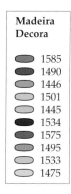

Madeira Decora

- 1585
- 1490
- 1446
- 1501
- 1445
- 1534
- 1575
- 1495
- 1533
- 1475

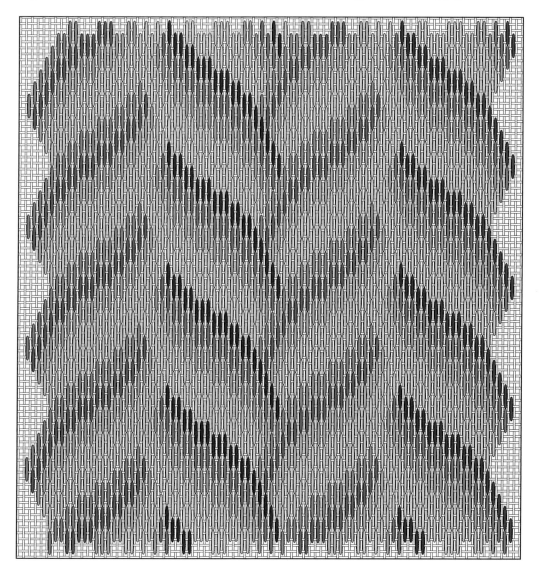

P U R P L E

*P*URPLE TONALITIES, especially violet and magenta, belong to the same color spectrum. Cleopatra's barge was claimed to navigate with purple sails. Deep purple robes were worn by the goddess Hera, wife of Zeus, and the Greek god Dionysus, as well as priests, emperors and bishops alike. While the violet of sweet lavender brought about sublime feelings, magenta offered supernatural powers. Known for their deep metaphysical and spiritual values, all these purple variations elevated feelings concerned with spiritual life and compassion for one another.

PURPLE

*"A weaver who has to direct and to interweave a great many
little threads has no time to philosophize about it, but rather
he is so absorbed in his work he doesn't think but acts, and he
feels how things must go more than he can explain it..."*

VINCENT VAN GOGH, LETTERS TO HIS BROTHER THEO

PURPLE, VIOLET AND MAGENTA all belong to the highest vibrations in the color spectrum, their difference being the dissimilar proportions of red and blue. Colors of spiritual intensity, they bring deep seeing and feeling into one's life. As mysterious and mystical colors, they hold hidden knowledge of the past and contain psychic vibrations of all things unseen. Balancing between heaven and earth, love and wisdom, passion and reason, these are colors concerned with searching for a spiritual love outside the everyday human experience.

Purple has always been used as an index of high appreciation and respect, representing the light of truth. Due to its exorbitant cost, genuine purple dye was once rare and precious and thus reserved for emperors and priests as the sign of luxury and affluence. A symbol of power and high rank, priests traditionally wore deep purple, known as royal purple, during the highest sacraments. Surrounded by an aura of goodness and righteousness, coupled with clarity of mind and sincere purpose, the color purple symbolized truth and justice. Being a deeper tone of violet mixed with blue, it brought forth the highest ideals in creative endeavors.

As an inspirational color, regal and dignified violet was considered the color of healing others, symbolizing contemplation that inspired the artistic and creative. Heightening inspiration, imagination and intuition, violet held clarity of focus and intense awareness of the higher realms. Its color enriched personal spaces where one could quietly meditate. A color helping in times of difficult change, violet vibrations burn negativity and make new growth possible. It represents sensitivity that knows the sadness of endings coupled with the joy of new beginnings. When choosing violet, one looks back on what has passed while standing on the threshold of the new. At such times the tendency to withdraw creates an inner calmness and tranquillity for difficult situations. Being a sensitive and meditative color it is highly personal and brings spiritual values into one's choices.

Magenta, the highest color vibration of all, combines violet and red energies and is the sacred color of divine love and divine healing. It stands for sacrificial love, the search for love beyond emotional desire where passion changes into compassion. Here one finds one's personal reason for living and then lives it. Its vibrations stimulate the ability to focus, bring about co-operation and deep caring for others. Reflecting the hidden power of the planet Scorpio, magenta moves from the material plane towards spiritual vision. Its elevated energy inspires enthusiasm, counteracting discouragement and despair. A vibrant color enabling one to release ideas, thought patterns and feelings no longer relevant, the magnetism of magenta attracts the unexpected that brings with it dynamic and vital challenges in life.

PEACOCK FEATHERS

Magenta is enhanced by turquoise as they both belong to the planet Uranus which brings the unexpected surprise of change after completing past responsibilities and is a far-reaching energy.

Here *Peacock Feathers* symbolizes the sacred bird spreading its tail as a cosmic wheel. Portraying the beauty and power of change, the peacock's plumage became radiant upon destroying the deadly serpent and transforming its poisons. Such a myth reinforces the magical and mysterious properties of magenta as it transmutes energy from an unknown source for its personal changes. The intensity of *Peacock Feathers* uses various upright stitches to create this energetic effect.

Magenta and turquoise carry knowledge of wisdom once known through deep intuitive sources. Its outrageous daring is the opposite of conservative beliefs. Here such vibrations are magnified by magenta and olive which address the wanderer, seeking a new direction for love, while re-evaluating life and looking within. Both gold and deep magenta bring an insight which radiates peace and delight.

Peacock Feathers, an elegant design of restraint and dignity, is reminiscent of past cultures as well as present day reality. It is symbolic and meaningful, evoking deep feelings and compassion for one's well-being. Its spiritual vibrations opens one's heart to others, embracing life with appreciation and acknowledgement of all that is beautiful and rewarding.

SKILL: advanced
CANVAS: Madeira 1282/70 antique 18 holes
NEEDLE: tapestry size 20
SIZE: 82 x 16.5 cm (32½ x 6½ in)

RIGHT: *An elegant and evocative design,* Peacock Feathers *belongs to the tradition of myth and memory, arousing feelings of an exotic bird with brilliant plumage. This complex pattern illustrates how bargello can be extended into new and imaginative realms through the use of dynamic colors and intricate stitching to create an energetic effect by combining traditional techniques with exciting interpretations.*

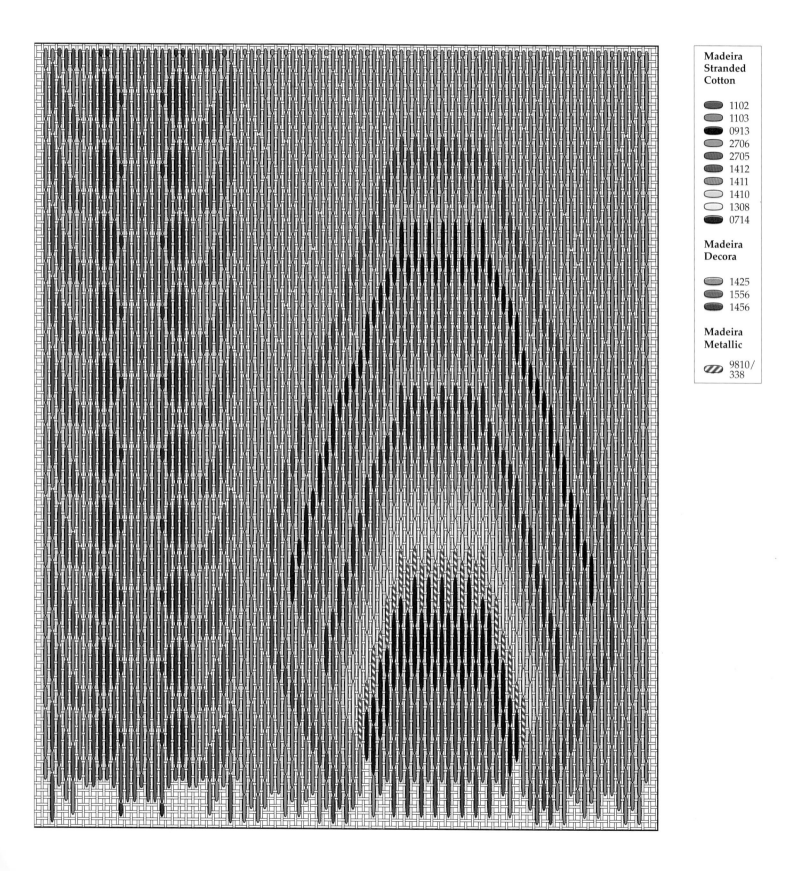

**Madeira
Stranded
Cotton**

- 1102
- 1103
- 0913
- 2706
- 2705
- 1412
- 1411
- 1410
- 1308
- 0714

**Madeira
Decora**

- 1425
- 1556
- 1456

**Madeira
Metallic**

- 9810/
  338

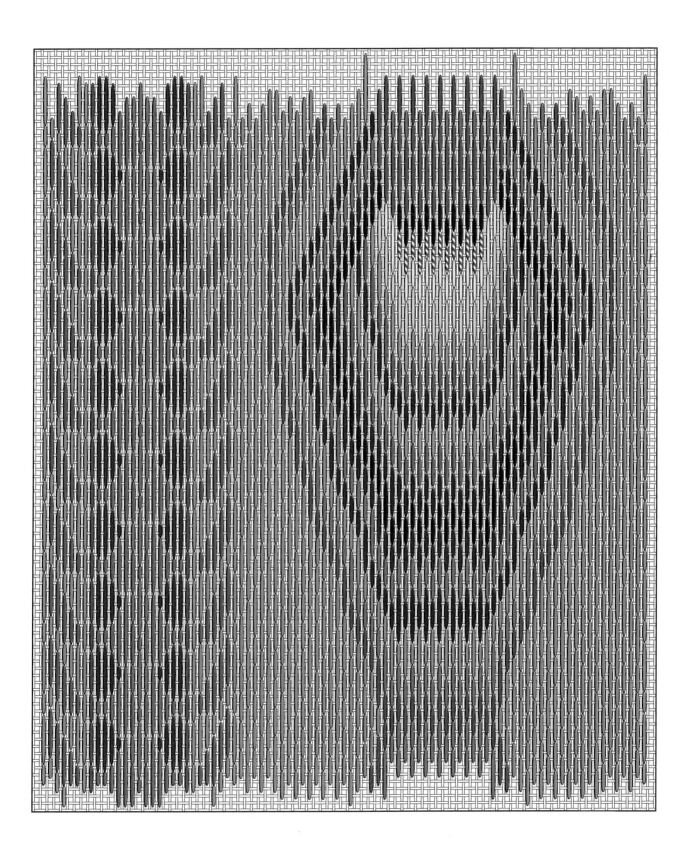

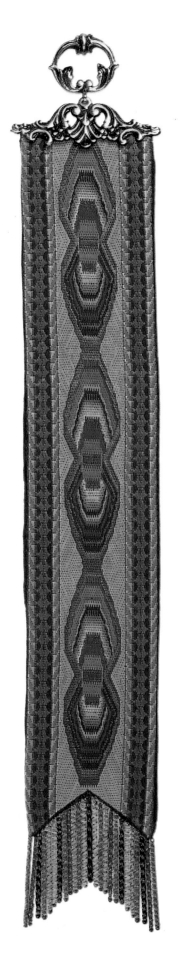

Yarn Quantities

Madeira Cotton		Metres
turquoise	1102	40
turquoise	1103	63
blue purple	0913	3
emerald	2706	7
emerald	2705	34
deep olive	1412	4
med olive	1411	5
light olive	1410	3
light olive	1308	3
purple	0714	40

Madeira Decora		
gold	1425	40
olive	1556	23
brown	1456	20

Madeira Metallic		
royal blue	9810/338	3

10 cm (4 in) coloured glass bobbins used as bottom fringe

CANVAS

◆ Cut the canvas to the desired size, allowing a border of 5 cm (2 in) all around for finishing.

◆ Tape or stitch all four sides to prevent fraying, *see Canvas, page 138* for details.

◆ Outline the approximate size and shape of the design with a tested, waterproof indelible ink marker. As a guideline draw a vertical line from the top center to the bottom.

◆ Using a blue fast-drying spray enamel paint, spray paint across the canvas surface to unify any color showing through.

FOLLOWING THE CHART

◆ This original design is challenging and complicated in pattern and requires careful attention in both the design and colors used.

◆ The stitch chart shows the basic design for this bell pull and should be repeated as many times as necessary to complete the example stitched. This pattern can be adjusted in length to any size preferred.

◆ Stitch this pattern from the top downwards, following the center motif as illustrated in both stitch charts. Then continue this repeated pattern until the bell pull is complete. The side borders should be stitched last.

STITCHING

◆ For detailed stitching instructions, *see Stitching, page 138*.

◆ Use Madeira Metallic, Madeira 6 Stranded Cotton and Madeira Decora as supplied (it is helpful to apply beeswax to the end of the Madeira Decora thread).

MAKING THE BELL PULL

◆ To obtain the brass top piece and colored glass bobbins for this bell pull, *see Suppliers' Addresses, page 141*. Here velvet has been used as the backing fabric and sewn to all four sides of the bell pull, allowing a small open seam at the top to slide through the brass top piece. The colored glass bobbins are sewn on last, taking care when hanging as they are very delicate.

SUNSHINE

Violet with hints of blue belongs to the planet Jupiter whose expansive, optimistic feelings are the secret of living fully. Violet is made from the devotion of blue coupled with the passion of red, creating a theme of nostalgic warmth. It is an inspirational color related to insight and love, as well as the self

respect and dignity held within ourselves. A passive color which absorbs light, the pale shades of violet are restful and serene, calming for all situations.

Here violet and green represent an individual coming from heart space, one who holds strong feelings for others, who sees both sides of a situation and makes the right decision, who gives freely yet remains independent. Violet and blue enhance this inspirational energy for they represent a person who nurtures and protects, is disciplined and uses intuition to see the overall perspective in each situation. As violet encourages relaxation in a dynamic rather than passive sense, it appreciates and supports tranquil and personal relationships.

In the deck chair *Sunshine*, such vitalizing and fresh energy motivates contemplation when in the quiet of open space, while the tonalities of brown help to ground intuitive energies as one interacts with others. In this place of repose and relaxation one enjoys the invigorating and challenging bargello pattern of *Sunshine*, whose subtle and sensuous energy attracts what one needs. Open to life's unfolding surprises, here one appears alone while receiving the attention of others, creating an interchange which is stimulating and most pleasurable.

SKILL: average
CANVAS: Madeira 1282/46 antique 12 holes
NEEDLE: tapestry size 16
SIZE: 40 x 112 cm (16 x 44 in)

RIGHT: *Intentionally vibrant and dynamic, this deck
chair reinterprets the sweep of a traditional
Florentine flame pattern in a broad and spacious way.
Here its design reflects the freedom of the
outdoors with its hot sun and cool evening breezes,
while the vibrant colors of purple and lilac are
reminiscent of summer flowers. The large stitches evoke
the energy of expansion, the pleasure which comes
from bringing creativity into life.*

Yarn Quantities

Madeira Viscona		Metres
lilac	1432	95
purple	1480	190
dark green	1479	83
med green	1450	83
light green	1447	43
dark blue	1496	100
med blue	1495	95
light blue	1446	100
brown	1542	90
brown	1456	83

CANVAS

◆ Cut the canvas to the desired size, allowing a border of 5 cm (2 in) all around for finishing.

◆ Tape or stitch all four sides to prevent fraying – *see Canvas, page 138* for details.

◆ Outline the size and shape of the design with a waterproof indelible marker.

◆ Using a blue fast-drying spray enamel paint, spray across the canvas surface to unify any color showing through.

FOLLOWING THE CHART

◆ This original design is a variation of traditional Florentine canvaswork that combines domes and spires, also known as scallops and flames. Its motif is uncomplicated as the first row establishes the pattern, all subsequent rows merely following.

◆ The stitch chart shows the basic design for this deck chair and should be repeated as many times as necessary to complete the example stitched. This pattern can be adjusted to any size or shape desired.

◆ As a single motif design, work each row from the right to left, beginning at the bottom right-hand corner until each horizontal row is completed.

STITCHING

◆ Because of the length of canvas used, roll the top part of the canvas and hold together with large clips, keeping free only the part being stitched. At the halfway point reverse the canvas, roll up the finished part, and complete the design.

◆ For detailed stitching instructions, *see Stitching, page 138.*

◆ Use Madeira Viscona doubled.

◆ This Madeira thread is only available in cones and must be specially ordered.

MAKING THE DECK CHAIR

◆ Lightly steam iron the canvas on the wrong side or block if needed. Machine-stitch to an

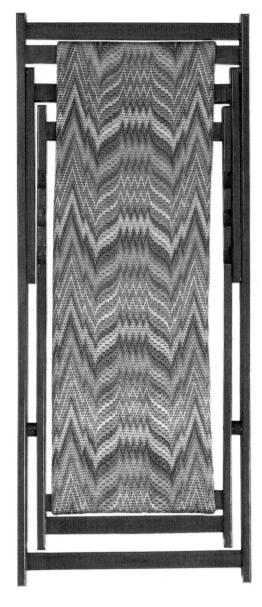

equal piece of outdoor green fabric, leaving space on both ends to insert the fixing pole of the deck chair.

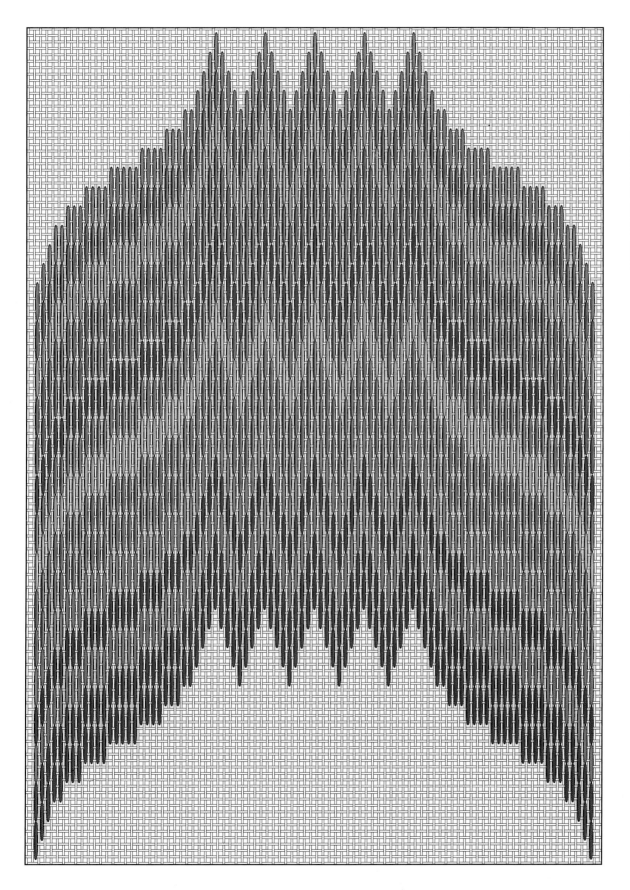

CELEBRATION

Celebration is an extravagant, wide-brimmed hat with charismatic and alluring colors that are regal and dignified, juxtaposed in an elegant and subtle manner. Its feminine mystery holds the secrets of someone living in the joyous moment of present time, open to fresh adventures. *Celebration* belongs to one making a strong, subtle and sensuous statement who, after releasing old behaviour patterns, now seeks total harmony with self.

Suggestive of sound intuition and potent psychic abilities, these sophisticated violet tones indicate an awareness that what is given to others is also received. Its stylised colors are a clear choice – there is nothing informal or accidental about them. Such violet and purple tones belong to one with loyalty and affection, a peace-loving person intrigued with playing different roles and using strong feminine intuition to help others.

Conscious of internal as well as external beauty, here the color grey is elusive and exclusive, indicating the beginning of a transformation. Black suggests detachment from the past, its respect and wisdom coming from a hidden source. Such presence makes the violet colors come alive, creates an atmosphere luxurious and intimate, and introduces a sense of drama with clear definition.

The design *Celebration* honors the dignity and grace that comes with wisdom and results from experience. Its bargello pattern makes an incredible statement, its design evoking courage and daring, as well as humor in the attention it attracts. A self-conscious creation of lightness and depth, *Celebration* adorns its wearer with bravura and commitment to life.

SKILL: average
CANVAS: Madeira 1282/70 antique 18 holes
NEEDLE: tapestry size 20
SIZE: hat size average/canvas size
43 x 43 cm (17 x 17 in)

RIGHT: *This wide brimmed hat is an extravagant celebration that is both individualistic and imaginative, its bargello pattern created from the center of the forehead outwards. The pleasurable sheen of silk enhances its dramatic quality as well as affording the lightness and flexibility of fabric ideal for making a hat.*

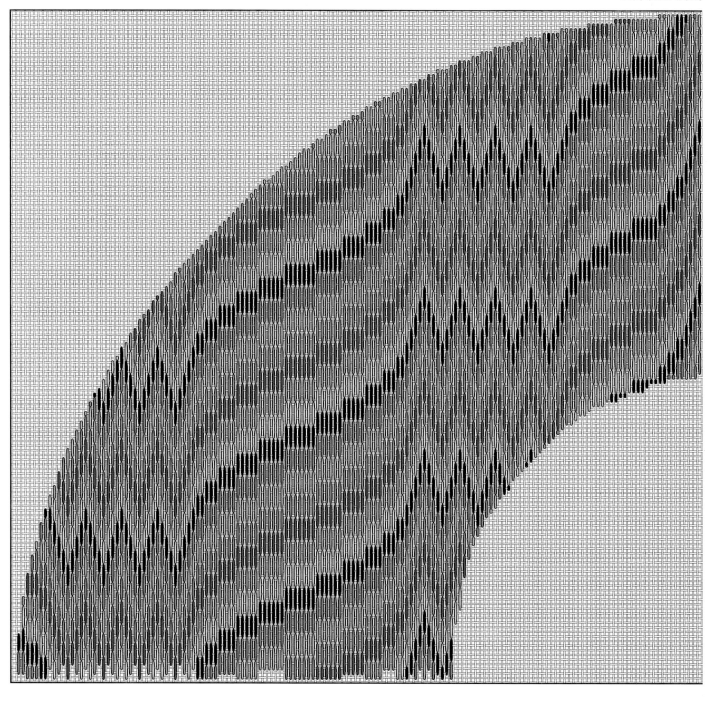

Hat brim front

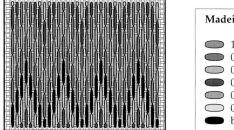

Hatband

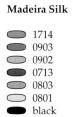

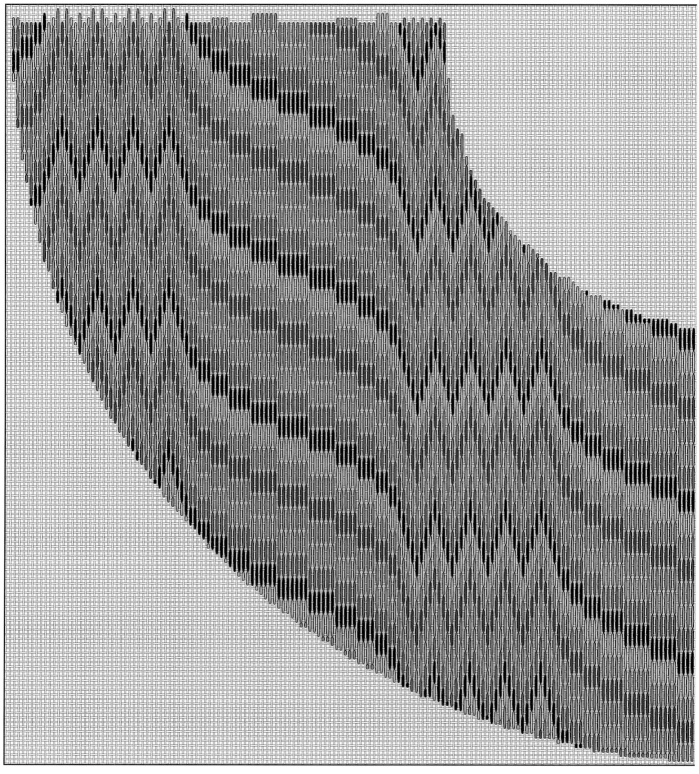

Hat brim back

129

Yarn Quantities

Madeira Silk		Metres
grey	1714	35
deep purple	0903	35
purple	0902	30
deep lilac	0713	30
med lilac	0803	30
light lilac	0801	25
black	black	25

CANVAS

◆ Cut a canvas square 50 x 50 cm (20 x 20 in). This allows for a border of 7.5 cm (3 in) all around for finishing.

◆ Tape or stitch all four sides to prevent fraying – *see Canvas, page 138* for details.

◆ Outline the approximate hat size of 43 x 43 cm (17 x 17 in) on the canvas with a tested, waterproof indelible ink marker, then draw central horizontal and vertical lines. At the design's center point, where these lines cross, draw an oval roughly 15 x 18 cm (6 x 7 in) for the head size.

◆ Using a blue fast-drying spray enamel paint, spray across the canvas surface to unify any color showing through.

FOLLOWING THE CHART

◆ This original design is a variation of traditional Florentine canvas work that combines domes and spires, also known as scallops and flames. Its motif is uncomplicated as once the pattern is established all subsequent rows follow.

◆ The stitch chart shows the basic design for this wide-brimmed hat and should be carefully followed to complete the example stitched. The center opening can be adjusted to any individual head size, the brim can be narrowed if so desired.

◆ Stitch each row from the right to left, beginning at the right side until that section is completed, then follow the same for the left side. The hat band is stitched separately.

STITCHING

◆ For detailed stitching instructions, *see Stitching, page 138.*

◆ Use Madeira Silk as supplied.

MAKING THE WIDE-BRIMMED HAT

◆ Unless you are skilled in hat-making, it is advisable to have this bargello pattern made up by a professional milliner – *see Suppliers' Addresses, page 141.*

RIBBONS

Against a lustrous black background, vibrant *Ribbons* of magenta and ochre play against one another. While magenta ribbons symbolize spiritual abundance, ochre ribbons represent earthly abundance. Elusive black supports its hidden secrets, evoking a treasure of drama and sophistication alluding to mystery rites and wisdom from the underworld.

These dynamic contrasting ribbons of magenta and ochre suggest transformation and the coming of new life. Releasing disappointments as one frees ideas and thought patterns no longer suitable in present time, the gradations from magenta to deep plum provide new energy in a gentle way. Detaching from what one loves, while still needing love, brings about melancholy. Once free, however, these liberated feelings permit one to move towards a more spiritual vision of life.

The warm tones from amber to deep ochre are reminiscent of the saffron robes of initiation when knowledge and intellect represent luminosity. These spheres, attuned to deep magenta spiritual thinking, access knowledge based on the wisdom of gold. Here, unhindered by obstacles, one discovers unknown creative possibilities through balancing intuition and reason.

The interaction of deep magenta with gold radiates profound pleasure, resolving problems created through confusion. Inspiring joy even during difficult times, one begins to include ancient wisdom in daily life, to embrace a greater capacity for happiness. This elevated energy creates a color vibration in *Ribbons* that brings enthusiasm and harmony during change as one stretches boundaries and opens to adventures beyond the scope of imagination.

SKILL: average
CANVAS: Madeira 1282/70 antique 18 holes
NEEDLE: tapestry size 20, bead size 22
SIZE: 40 x 34 cm (16 x 13½ in)

Yarn Quantities

Madeira Cotton		Metres
gold	2514	10
ochre	2302	20
rust brown	2306	10
rust brown	2305	20
red	0513	20
crimson	0705	40
deep red	0602	20
crimson	2608	40
Madeira Decora		
black	1400	190

CANVAS

◆ Cut the canvas to the desired size, allowing a border of 5 cm (2 in) all around for finishing. Bind the edges – *see Canvas, page 138* for details.

◆ Outline the size and shape of the design with a waterproof indelible marker, then draw central horizontal and vertical lines. The design's center point is where these lines cross.

◆ Using a deep brown fast-drying spray enamel paint, spray across the canvas surface to unify any color showing through.

FOLLOWING THE CHART

◆ This ribbon design is a variation of a traditional bargello pattern. The pattern is uncomplicated but needs close concentration to begin the basic lines.

◆ After creating four parallel stitch lines in undulating rows, which interlock with similar undulating rows from another direction, the pattern is established. The black curved diamond sections in-between strongly enhance its dramatic multi-dimensional effect.

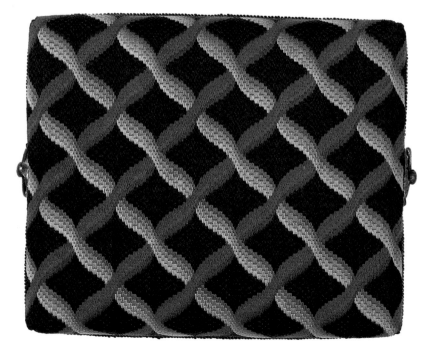

◆ The stitch chart shows the basic design for this footstool, to be repeated as many times as necessary until completed. This pattern can be adjusted to any size or shape desired.

◆ Thread eight needles with the complete color sequence, i.e. four variations of magenta and four variations of ochre, graduated from light to dark.

◆ Begin at the center of the canvas and work outwards, stitching all four stitches of each undulating section until its sequence is established. The colors that are not being used should be placed to the right of the design so as not to interfere with the stitching thread. By keeping these other threads at the front they will not become tangled at the back.

◆ After completing the center section, stitch the border pattern; each is a separate section.

STITCHING

◆ For instructions, *see Stitching, page 138.*

◆ When the stitching is complete, sew on the black glass beads individually – *see Beading, page 139.*

◆ Use Madeira 6 Stranded Cotton as supplied. Use Madeira Decora doubled.

◆ The quantities stated include the border.

MAKING THE FOOTSTOOL

◆ This pattern can be adjusted to any rectangular footstool chosen with the recommendation that it be finished by a professional upholsterer – *see Suppliers' Addresses, page 141.*

R I G H T : *Created for a Victorian footstool, this bargello pattern is well suited to any size as its design can be adjusted accordingly. Such flexibility of bargello canvaswork allows you to cover personal items of similar or dissimilar size, with the added elegance of glass beads to separate the space between its border and main pattern.*

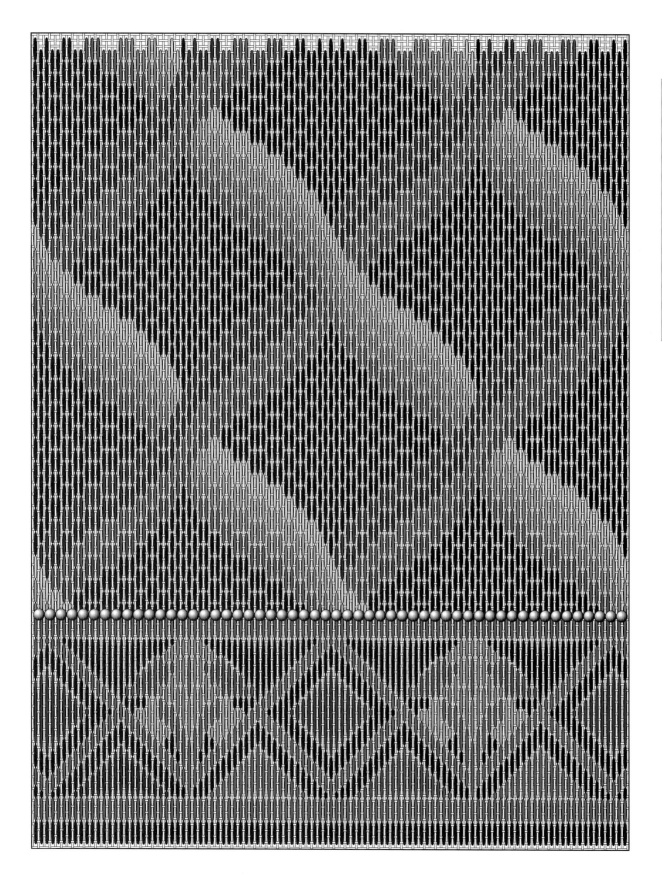

J E W E L

The reds and purples of this intimate cushion magnetically draw attention to its intense energy. Its powerful color combination radiates and receives love, encourages dedication and elevates self-esteem. On a psychic and material level, it brings peace and freshness to life. Mysterious black, the

explorer of the unknown, accentuates its brilliant jewel-like qualities.

The supporting colors of violet and turquoise suggest visionary qualities that help to decipher dreams and develop extrasensory perception while exploring new possibilities relating to one's personal and public life. Violet and turquoise seek and pursue challenges with integrity and maturity. Creating harmony in relationships while remaining aware of self-deception, its honesty and charisma enhance the joy of new possibilities.

The colors of magenta and turquoise love beauty everywhere, embrace compassion and unconditional love, carefully planning events so they are wonderful and pleasant. Being creative and determined, here one loves the successful completion of a project. Able to distance from problems and entanglements, enthusiastic emotions inspire a new focus while awareness of detail and precision permits things to be seen from an unusual perspective. The passionate side of violet and red encourages progressive ideas. Using clairvoyance and clarity, thoughts stay in heaven while one's feet remain on earth. Exploring the love of freedom stimulates new energy and productivity. The magic of the *Jewel* cushion is the interaction and integration of these exciting combinations.

SKILL: average
CANVAS: Madeira 1282/70 antique 18 holes
NEEDLE: tapestry size 20
SIZE: 37 x 26 cm (14½ x 10½ in)

OVERLEAF: *As well as featuring a classic three-dimensional bargello pattern, this small cushion is stitched with a mixture of single and double threads to enhance its complexity. Through the use of black metallic threads, its purple tones richly shimmer throughout the design. The effect of* Jewel *is of a cushion small and precious yet potent enough to make a statement of its own.*

Yarn Quantities

Madeira Decora		Metres
turquoise	1585	10
green	1580	17
black	1400	31
purple	1522	27
red	1439	28
rust	1435	23
lilac	1480	17

Madeira Lame Metallic		
black	9814/470	20

CANVAS

◆ Cut the canvas, allowing a border of 5 cm (2 in) all around for finishing. Bind the edges – *see Canvas, page 138* for details.

◆ Outline the size and shape of the design with a waterproof indelible marker, allowing for the edging as well.

◆ Spray paint the canvas deep red to unify any color showing through.

FOLLOWING THE CHART

◆ This adaptation of classic eighteenth-century Florentine patterns, consisting of one continuous line interspersed with other lines broken, is found in many variations. Here its effect is dramatically altered by the colors and metallic threads being used.

◆ The chart shows the basic design and should be repeated as necessary to complete the example stitched. This pattern can be adjusted to any size or shape.

STITCHING

◆ Begin at the bottom right-hand side of the chart first and establish the black semi-circular lines to complete one horizontal row. Next, choose another color related to this horizontal row and complete that.

◆ Then select the next color continuing in this fashion until the pattern is completed. The black metallic threads are best stitched last.

◆ After finishing the lower half of the stitching, reverse the canvas to complete the upper half. Then stitch the black border around the design, as well as its black metallic trim.

◆ For detailed stitching instructions, *see Stitching, page 138.*

◆ Use Madeira Decora as supplied (it is helpful to apply beeswax to the end of the Decora thread). Use Madeira Lame Metallic doubled.

MAKING THE CUSHION

◆ To complete the cushion, *see Finishing instructions, page 139.*

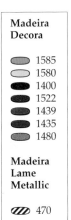

Madeira Decora

- ⬭ 1585
- ⬭ 1580
- ⬭ 1400
- ⬭ 1522
- ⬭ 1439
- ⬭ 1435
- ⬭ 1480

Madeira Lame Metallic

⬭ 470

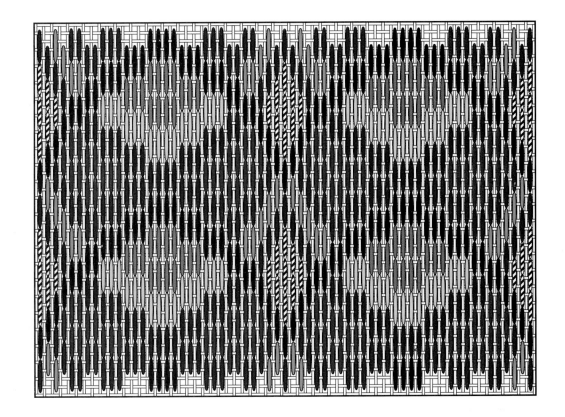

MATERIALS AND TECHNIQUES

YARNS

As dye lots vary, purchase all yarns together to assure the same color match and check that they are colorfast. Choose colors in daylight as artificial light changes both color and tone. When possible, purchase hanks rather than skeins as this is more economical.

Traditionally the criterion for choosing yarns has been whether they produced an even, hard-wearing fabric. However, with the extensive variety of threads now available, it is often more creative to expand one's skills, such experimentation adding another dimension to the dramatic effect of bargello patterns. The thickness of threads selected must be proportional to the canvas mesh size so the surface remains fully covered. Fine threads can be doubled, and thick threads can sometimes be separated.

CANVAS

Use single mono de luxe canvas which has evenly spaced warp and weft threads, the mesh sizes being determined by the amount of holes per inch. Use the finest quality canvas available to assure no knots or flaws, as well as the accuracy of holes per inch. In lesser quality a 13 and 14 mesh canvas can have 13½ holes, making a difference to the finished design size.

When measuring the canvas size, allow for the final stitching to shrink the canvas slightly and allow a border of 5 cm (2 in) all round for finishing. After cutting the canvas to size, bind, sew or machine stitch the cut edges or use adhesive sticky tape, even surgical tape which holds extremely well, to prevent fraying.

Before stitching, spray the canvas with a fast-drying enamel spray paint to unify any color showing through after the design has been stitched.

It is unnecessary to use a frame as upright stitches create very little canvas distortion. If desired, only rectangular frames are suggested as round frames distort the canvas itself. Ideal for single thread stitching, 18 hole mono canvas comes in many colors, including red, blue, green etc. This special order canvas is available from Beautiful Bargello Ltd (see page 140).

When not stitching, always roll the canvas, design outwards, to avoid distortion from folding.

STITCHING

When stitching bargello it is traditional to count the canvas threads being covered rather than the holes. Keep stitches in a light, even tension which covers the canvas well, stitching one complete row at a time (when possible) before starting the next color, using threads approximately 45 cm (18 in) long. After threading a tapestry needle there are two different methods used to begin stitching:

a) The thread may be temporarily knotted passing from front to back at least 3.5 cm (1½ in) to the left of the row being stitched. These threads are worked into the stitching itself, the knot being clipped after the threads have been intertwined.

b) Another stitching method begins and finishes the threads by sewing them through the back of existing stitches at least 2.5 cm (1 in) in length, preferably using two directions with Decora Viscose thread to prevent it from loosening.

Avoid using knots as they tend to unravel. Clip thread ends short on the back of the canvas, as well as ends pulled through to the front during stitching.

Should threads become twisted, either let the needle swing free or lightly run the threads between your fingernails to clear any unevenness.

When starting a new bargello design, decide which part of the canvas is to be the center and begin there. From the center work to the left, then to the right, completing one row.

Other Bargello patterns vary in placement:

a) Single line motifs are generally worked from the right to left, from the bottom right-hand corner upwards.

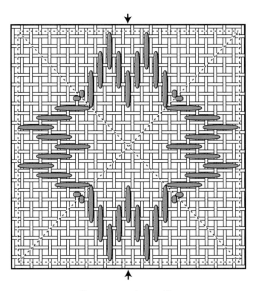

Four-way bargello

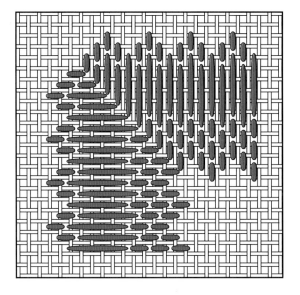

A mitred corner

b) Trellis type patterns benefit most from beginning in the canvas center and stitching outwards until the pattern is established.

c) The right angle of a border design needs to be established first to ensure that the border design meets, then the pattern within is stitched.

Should a bargello pattern become irregular, correct the error by placing a needle under each consecutive stitch and pulling out until the mistake is found, then begin anew with a fresh thread. If part of a stitch has been missed, go over it rather than rip out. Should the clearing of mistakes necessitate cutting threads, clean any frayed thread ends with adhesive tape.

For clarity and convenience keep all colors in their proper sequence:

a) When using packs of threads, hold them in order with a large paper clip or a rubber band.

b) Loose yarns can be placed in a palette made from stiff card with holes punched for each color used.

The quantities of threads given throughout this book are approximate and will vary from person to person. All bargello patterns within the book need to be stitched upon the canvas size specified, otherwise the finished piece will be different from that shown.

When reading the bargello charts within this book the lines on both sides of the thread represent the lines on the actual canvas to be crossed.

Various threads are used double on canvas of 13, 14, and 15 holes. If you prefer single threads then use canvas of 18 holes. The height remains the same only the width will be approximately 10 cm (4 in) narrower, therefore adjust the design accordingly.

BEADING

As with yarn, dye lots vary so purchase all your beads together to assure the same color match. Each glass bead equals one single stitch and is applied separately onto the design with an upright stitch over two threads of canvas. Use a double thickness of either synthetic or beeswaxed sewing thread as glass beads tend to cut cotton, silk or wool threads. Only apply beads when stitching is complete.

FINISHING

After finishing, color photocopy your completed work. This process is invaluable should you later decide to make a second complementary design, either as a mirror image or an enlargement of a section.

Often blocking is not necessary for bargello work. If desired the traditional method of blocking should be used. For a smooth, even surface, lightly steam iron the finished piece on its reverse side.

Before making up, hold the completed canvas to the light to see if any stitches are missing. Also, add one additional row in a toning color around the entire design and later machine sew between this edge and the finished design.

Bargello cushions require some sewing skill but are not difficult to make. They either can be knife edged or box cushions, the backing fabric according to personal taste. Machine stitch together the chosen backing fabric and completed bargello work on three sides, right sides facing, stitching between the completed canvaswork and additional stitched row. When finished, turn the cushion right side up, insert a muslin covered pad and close either by hand stitching or inserting a zip. Hand sew either tasselled or plain fringe, cord, crochet edging or any other desired trim.

Unless you are extremely skilled in finishing work a completed chair seat cover, a vest (waistcoat), a wide-brimmed hat, a mirrored frame etc. should be made up professionally, thus assuring that the stitching will be finished properly in the manner deserved. Finished work always should be dry cleaned to preserve the quality of its threads, as well as preventing unnecessary shrinking from hand washing.

STRETCHING, BACKING, MAKING UP

Beautiful Bargello Ltd provides all the services needed to complete the projects within this book. Cushions can be stretched and made up with trimming and fabric, furniture pieces upholstered and made up, the wide-brimmed hat made to measure, the carpet bag, lampshade and waistcoat finished and lined, the wall mirror framed, and so on. For further information, contact Beautiful Bargello Ltd at the above address.

KITS FROM BEAUTIFUL BARGELLO LTD

The following Joyce Petschek designs illustrated in this book are available as kits:

page		
17	344	*Mosaics* cushion
19	337	*Thistle II* cushion
22/23	339/40	*Harmony I/II* pair footstools/cushions
26	320	*Gypsy Carpet Bag*
45	329	*Exotica* bolster
47	318	*Italia* oblong cushion
58	321	*Lattice* brick door stop
70	315	*Trees* cushion
90	319	*Byzantine* oblong cushion
106/107	322	*Gambler's Delight* waistcoat
101	310	*Garland* oblong cushion
127	326	*Celebration* wide-brimmed hat
133	331	*Ribbons* footstool/cushion

The kits, as well as threads, canvas and accessories, are obtainable by mail order from the following addresses:

Beautiful Bargello Ltd
Leandown House
7 Nestles Avenue
Hayes
Middlesex UB3 4SA
tel: 0181 756 1080
fax: 0181 756 1090

SCS
9631 North East Colfax
Portland
Oregon 97220
tel: 800 547 8025 or 503 252 1452
fax: 503 252 7280

SOURCES AND SUPPLIERS

MADEIRA

Six-stranded cotton, Silk, Decora, Renaissance Wool, Viscona, Lurana and Metallic have been used for all the bargello patterns in this book. Madeira threads are available worldwide. For your local stockist, contact the following Madeira distributors:

UNITED KINGDOM

Madeira Threads (UK) Ltd
Thirsk Industrial Park
York Road
Thirsk
North Yorkshire YO7 3BX
tel: 01845 524880
fax: 01845 525046

Barnyarns Ltd
PO Box 28
Thirsk
North Yorkshire YO7 3YN
tel: 01845 524344
mail order only

UNITED STATES

SCS
9631 North East Colfax
Portland
Oregon 97220
tel: 800 547 8025/503 252 1452
fax: 503 252 7280

ASIA

Madeira Asia PTE Ltd
3 Maritime Square
11/01/01 Cable Car Towers
Singapore 099254
tel: 65 278 0006
fax: 65 278 0004

AUSTRALIA

Penguin Threads (PTY) Ltd
25/27 Izett Street
Prahran
Victoria 3181
tel: 613 529 4400
fax: 613 525 1172

GERMANY

Madeira Garne
U & M Schmidt & Co GmbH
Hans-Bunte-Strasse 8
79003 Freiburg
tel: 0761 510480
fax: 0761 502342

ITALY

Micheleti C. SPA
Via Desiderio 25
1/20131 Milan
tel: 392 266 3553
fax: 392 266 4158

JAPAN

Madeira Japan Ltd
15-37 Funahashi-cho
Tennoji-ku
Osaka 543
tel: 816 765 1300
fax: 816 764 6087

SOUTH AFRICA

Madeira Threads (SA)
PO Box 168
Witfield 1467
tel: 2711 976 2571
fax: 2711 393 3985

SPAIN

M. Sorribes-Cugat
c/Fortia Casanovas
12 BJOS DCHA
Barcelona 08850/Gava
tel: 343 638 1666
fax: 343 638 1869

DMC

UNITED KINGDOM

DMC Creative World
Pullman Road
Wigston
Leicestershire LE18 2DY
tel: 0116 281 1040
fax: 0116 281 3592

UNITED STATES

The DMC Corporation
Port Kearny
Building 10
South Kearny NJ 07032
tel: 201 589 0606
fax: 201 589 8931

AUSTRALIA

DMC Needlecraft Pty Ltd
51-66 Carrington Road
Marrickville NSW 2204
tel: 612 559 3088
fax: 612 559 5338

BENELUX

DMC
7/9 Rue de Pavillion
B-1210 Brussels
tel: 322 216 9145
fax: 322 245 1707

FRANCE

DMC
10 avenue Ladru-Rollin
75579 Paris Cedex 12
tel: 331 4928 1000
fax: 331 4342 5191

ITALY

DMC
Viale Italia 84
I-20020 Lainate Mi
tel: 392 935 70427 or 28, 29
fax: 392 935 70398

PORTUGAL

DMC
Travessa da Escola
Araujo 36-A
P-1100 Lisbon
tel: 351 135 60311
fax: 351 135 56788

SCANDINAVIA

DMC
Dampfaergevej 8
Frihavnen
DK-2100 Copenhagen
tel: 453 526 2211
fax: 453 526 2812

SPAIN

DMC
Fontanella 21-23
(Floors 4 & 5)
E-08010 Barcelona
tel: 343 317 7440
fax: 343 302 5023

SWITZERLAND

DMC
Morgenstreasse 1
CH 9242 Oberuzwit SG
tel: 417 351 1515
fax: 417 351 2797

The following stockists have kindly supplied materials for this book:

GLASS BEADS AND GLASS BOBBINS

The Brighton Bead Shop
21 Sydney Street
Brighton, BN1 4EN
tel: 01273 675077

B & M Tuffnell
Navenby
Westgate
Driffield YO25 7LJ
East Yorkshire
tel: 01377 240745

TRIMMINGS AND FABRICS

M & J Trimming Co Inc
1000 Sixth Avenue
New York NY 10018
tel: 212 391 6200

Osborne and Little plc
49 Temperley Road
London SW12 8QE
tel: 0181 675 2255 (for details of stockists)

Osborne and Little Inc
90 Commerce Road
Stamford
Connecticut 06902
tel: 203 359 1500

YARN QUANTITIES

Ambrosia, p.14

	DMC Perle	DMC Cotton	Metres
light mauve		2316	20
med mauve		2328	20
deep mauve		2398	70
light brown		2302	20
rose brown		2405	20
med brown		2632	70
light grey	415		18
med grey	414		15
dark grey	413		70

Use DMC 6 Stranded Cotton doubled.
Use DMC Coton Perle No.3 as supplied.

Thistle, p.17

	DMC Wool	Metres
turquoise	7956	33
deep green	7540	25
crimson	7212	33
mauve	7210	33
rust	7875	28
apricot	7360	30
purple	7257	33
deep lilac	7255	23

Needlepoint Border:

			Metres
turquoise	993		10
deep green	991		9
deep lilac	554		10
crimson	815		8
rust	351		17
apricot	920		6

Use DMC Wool as supplied.

Harmony I, p.20

	DMC Perle	DMC Cotton	Metres
brown		2801	20
brown		2299	20
brown		2400	20
brown		2918	20
red		2902	20
red		2346	20
red		2237	20
red		3830	20
red		2345	20
deep crimson	815		50
deep brown	918		40
copper	920		3

Use DMC Coton Perle and DMC 6 Stranded Cotton as supplied.

Reflections, p.34

	DMC Perle	DMC Metallic	Metres
deep gold	783		75
med gold	762		65
yellow	726		45
med gold	729		115
light gold	725		70
gold		art.284	60

Use three threads of DMC Embroidery metallic. Use DMC Coton Perle No.3 as supplied.

Harmony II, p.20

	DMC Perle	DMC Cotton	Metres
brown		2801	20
brown		2299	20
brown		2400	20
brown		2918	20
red		2902	20
red		2346	20
red		2237	20
red		3830	10
red		2345	20
crimson	815		50
deep brown	918		40
copper	920		3

Use DMC Coton Perle and DMC 6 Stranded Cotton as supplied.

Gipsy Carpet Bag, p.25

	DMC Perle	DMC Wool	Metres
deep green		7429	150
deep blue		7384	175
deep gold		7782	95
med gold		7783	80
light gold		7484	45
med red		7127	175
rose		7146	125
taupe brown		7801	350
brown		434	475

Use DMC Tapestry Wool and DMC Coton Perle as supplied.

Russian Music, p.38

	DMC Perle	DMC Metallic	Metres
gold	783		75
rust	918		63
rust	223		75
brown	732		88
red	498		105
rust	356		48
black	310		98
black		art.271	148

Use four threads of DMC Embroidery metallic doubled. Use DMC Coton Perle No.3 as supplied.

Exotica, p.43

	DMC Perle	DMC Cotton	Metres
deep rust		2921	20
rust		2766	70
deep gold		2765	80
light gold		2436	20
mauve		2328	180
rust	796		110
copper	3685		70
rust	301		28

Use DMC Coton Perle No.3 and DMC Cotton doubled.

Italia, p.46

	DMC Perle	DMC Cotton	Metres
med green		2138	40
dark green		2500	48
mauve		2328	20
mauve		2398	80
purple		2394	48
rust		3803	48
crimson		2570	48
green		2137	20
brown		2400	52
burgundy	815		39
gold	782		79

Use DMC Coton Perle as supplied.
Use DMC 6 Stranded Cotton doubled.

Renaissance pelmet, p.64

	DMC Perle	DMC Metallic	Metres
mauve	221		200
deep rust	920		100
med. rust	356		220
dark green	991		220
deep olive	987		260
med olive	3347		280
deep mauve	221		200
apricot	351		100
blue	797		240
gold	783		100
deep rose	3328		80
burgundy	902		100
deep green	890		180
blue	796		260
gold	782		120
burnt gold		art.273	1008

Use DMC Coton Perle No.3 as supplied.
Use three strands of DMC Metallic doubled.

Renaissance tieback, p.64

	DMC Perle	DMC Metallic	Metres
deep mauve	221		17
deep rust	920		17
med rust	356		8
dark green	991		10
deep olive	987		10
med olive	3347		10
med mauve	223		13
apricot	351		8
sapphire blue	797		8
gold	783		40
terracotta	975		40
deep rose	3328		8
burgundy	902		8
deep green	890		10
deep blue	796		10
deep rust	782		25
burnt gold		art.273	6

Use DMC Coton Perle No.3 as supplied
Use three strands of DMC Metallic doubled.

Stained Glass, p.54

	DMC Perle	DMC Wool	DMC Metallic	Metres
brown	801			75
red	498			38
light green		7927		13
med green		7320		13
dark green		7701		25
light blue		7283		25
med blue		7306		13
med red		7666		25
deep red		7107		25
crimson		7038		13
gold			art 284	660

Use four threads of DMC Embroidery Metallic doubled. Use DMC Tapestry wool and DMC Coton Perle No.3 as supplied.

Lattice, p.57

	DMC Cotton	Metres
aubergine	3803	20
crimson	2570	20
dark pink	2916	30
deep lilac	2718	20
dusty pink	2572	20
red	2103	30
deep red	2110	30
deep red	2346	30
dark red	2815	30

Use DMC 6 Stranded Cotton as supplied.

Phoenix, p.60

	DMC Perle	DMC Cotton	DMC Wool	Metres
red		2103		40
red		2110		18
coral		2815		15
orange		2350		20
apricot		2666		20
orange		2570		10
burnt orange		2918		13
brown	918			160
crimson			7138	25
copper	920			50

Use DMC Tapestry Wool and DMC Coton Perle No.3 as supplied.

Autumn, p.76

	DMC Cotton	DMC Wool	DMC Metallic	Metres
deep green		7541		38
med green		7320		25
aubergine		7259		38
deep olive		7427		25
med olive		7988		25
light green		7384		63
light olive		7547		63
deep rust	2815			18
crimson	2902			15
crimson	3803			18
greens			art.269	257

Use DMC Coton Perle No.3 and DMC Tapestry wool as supplied. Use DMC Embroidery Metallic three times doubled.

Trees, p.69

	DMC Wool	Metres
light gold	7472	12.5
gold	7785	6.5
gold	7484	25
gold	7782	25
dark gold	7444	37.5
light green	7323	12.5
green	7927	25
green	7324	25
green	7320	6.5
dark green	7541	37.5
light blue	7301	6.5
blue	7800	12.5
blue	7283	25
blue	7304	25
dark blue	7306	37.5
light red	7850	6.5
red	7127	12.5
red	7303	25
red	7107	25
dark red	7138	37.5

Use DMC Tapestry Wool as supplied.

Springtime, p.83

	DMC Perle	Metres
dark green	890	35
dark green	3346	30
dark green	3345	25
dark green	987	30
light green	913	15
med green	911	15
red	3687	5
red	900	5
red	666	5
red	815	5
lilac	554	5
lilac	208	5
lilac	799	5
lilac	210	5
terracotta	632	5
terracotta	902	5
terracotta	356	5
terracotta	224	5
gold	352	5
gold	223	5
gold	402	5
gold	725	5

Use DMC Coton Perle No.3 as supplied.

Florentine Flower, p.96

	DMC Perle	Metres
light green	223	8
med green	702	3
dark green	991	10
deep rose	223	10
red	815	13
burgundy	902	40
lilac	553	10
purple	550	65
med blue	796	10
dark blue	322	70

Use DMC Coton Perle No.3 as supplied.

Emerald Maze, p.80

	DMC Perle	Metres
light green	890	10
green	699	10
green	701	10
light green	702	10
dark green	732	10
green	580	10
green	581	10
light green	471	10

Use DMC Coton Perle No.3 as supplied.

Byzantine, p.88

	DMC Perle	DMC Metallic	Metres
blue	322		5
deep blue	930		15
red	498		13
mauve	356		5
dark green	890		43
green	991		48
olive green	3345		43
olive	3346		40
brown	829		18
light green	642		33
gold		art.284	560

Use four threads of DMC Metallic doubled. Use DMC Coton Perle No.3 as supplied.

Garland, p.100

	DMC Perle	Metres
red	498	50
rust	356	33
grey blue	930	28
med blue grey	322	28
light blue grey	518	28
dark green	991	20
med green	320	10
deep green	890	28
med olive	3345	28
light olive	3346	28
deep blue	798	20
dark blue	813	10

Use DMC Coton Perle No.3 as supplied.

Peacock Feathers, p.116

	DMC Perle	DMC Cotton	Metres
turquoise		2995	40
turquoise		2996	63
blue purple		2820	3
emerald		2956	7
emerald		2132	34
deep olive		2937	4
med olive		2469	5
light olive		2347	3
light olive		2907	3
purple		2394	40
royal blue	336		3

Use DMC 6 Stranded Cotton and DMC Coton Perle No.3 as supplied.

Gambler's Delight, p.104

	DMC Perle	DMC Metallic	Metres
turquoise	995		35
med blue	826		40
grey blue	797		40
med. blue	518		45
black	310		60
red	498		65
gold		art.284	180

Use DMC Coton Perle No.3 as supplied. Use three threads of DMC Embroidery Metallic doubled.

Twists, p.109

	DMC Perle	Metres
aqua dark	993	57
aqua	991	57
aqua	807	57
aqua	913	57
light aqua	955	57
dark blue	336	64
blue	798	64
blue	996	64
blue	799	64
light blue	827	64

Use Madeira Decora and DMC Coton Perle No 3 as supplied.

Sunshine, p.121

	DMC Perle	Metres
lilac	208	95
purple	552	190
dark green	909	83
med green	912	83
light green	913	43
dark blue	995	100
med blue	996	95
light blue	943	100
brown	780	90
brown	829	83

Use DMC Coton Perle No.3 doubled.

Celebration, p.126

	DMC Perle	Metres
grey	413	35
deep purple	550	35
purple	208	30
deep lilac	553	30
med lilac	554	30
light lilac	210	25
black	310	25

Use DMC Coton Perle No.3 as supplied.

Ribbons, p.131

	DMC Perle	DMC Cotton	Metres
gold		2783	10
ochre		2766	20
rust brown		2921	10
rust brown		2918	20
red		2110	20
crimson		2916	40
deep red		2570	20
crimson		2902	40
black	310		95

Use DMC 6 Strand Cotton and DMC Coton Perle No.3 as supplied.

Jewel, p.135

	DMC Perle	DMC Metallic	Metres
turquoise	943		10
green	471		17
black	310		31
purple	550		27
red	498		28
rust	902		23
lilac	552		17
black		art.271	60

Use DMC Coton Perle No.3 as supplied. Use three threads of DMC Embroidery Metallic doubled.

BIBLIOGRAPHY

Ashley, Laura, *The Colour Book*, Ebury Press, London, 1995 • Boyles, Margaret, *Bargello, An Explosion in Color*, MacMillan Publishing Co., New York, 1974 • Dalichow, Irene and Booth, Mike, *Aura-Soma*, Hay House, Inc., California 1996 • Fischer, Pauline and Lasker, Anabel, *Bargello Magic*, J.M.Dent and Sons, London, 1972 • Gage, John, *Colour and Culture*, Thames and Hudson, London, 1995 • Guild, Tricia, *Tricia Guild on Colour*, Conran Octopus, London, 1995 • Kaestner, Dorothy, *Needlepoint Bargello*, Bell & Hyman, London, 1974, 1985 reprint • Kaestner, Dorothy, *Four Way Bargello*, Bell & Hyman, London, 1968 • Kennett, Frances and Scarlett, Belinda, *Traditional Needlepoint*, Conran Octopus, London, 1988 • Phelan, Dorothy, *Florentine Canvaswork*, B.T .Batsford Ltd., London, 1991 • Roskill, Mark, *Vincent Van Gogh – Letters to his Brother Theo*, HarperCollins Publishers, London • Sloan, Annie and Gwynn, Kate, *Colour in Decoration*, Frances Lincoln, London, 1990 • Snook, Barbara, *Florentine Embroidery*, Charles Scribner's Sons, New York, 1967 • Theroux, Alexander, *The Primary Colors*, Henry Holt and Co., New York, 1994 • Williams, Elsa S., *Bargello, Florentine Canvas Work*, Reinhold Publishing Corp., New York, 1967

INDEX

AUTHOR'S ACKNOWLEDGEMENTS

My sincere appreciation to Madeira Threads (UK) Ltd for supplying the extensive variety of threads and canvas used in this book. A special thank you to its director, Ian MacPherson and his wife Sara, to Heather Montgomerie and Helen Metcalfe for their continual helpfulness and to Richard Tavener for the original introduction. My thanks to B&M Tuffnell for their exquisite glass bobbins, to Osborne & Little for their fabrics and furnishings, to the Brighton Bead Shop for their Venetian glass beads.

My admiration and gratitude to all the incredible stitchers involved: Carla Petschek, Ilda Santos, Jill Powell, Anne Hyne, Helen Day, Jackie Hughes, Doreen James, Elfrieda Jones, Eunice Williams, Kate Haxell, Muna Reyal, Jean Dowling, Liz Drury, Jackie Lobig, Alice Nicol, Felicity Mee, Pat Mitchenall.

My appreciation to Heini Schneebeli for his exquisite photography, my admiration to Deborah Schneebeli Morrell for her beautiful arrangements of the objects. My gratefulness to Michael Samuelson for his consistent generosity allowing the use of his narrow boat for photography, as well as to Pamela Watts for lending her beaded bags for photography. A special thank you to Deborah Wadham for her expertise in making up the wide-brimmed hat. My appreciation always to Fae Longman for her computer knowledge, to Sandra Bartu for her wisdom concerning Aura Soma color, to Ethan Danielson for his meticulous stitch charts.

A special thanks to my literary agent, Evelyne Duval, for her patience and persistence. My gratefulness to all those wondrous persons associated with Collins & Brown, particularly to Cindy Richards who commissioned this project, to Kate Haxell for her dedication and commitment to every detail, to Muna Reyal for her helpfulness, to Janet James for her handsome layouts, to Gillian Haslam for her clarity.